THE 5 HABITS OF

PRAYERFUL

PEOPLE

"*The 5 Habits of Prayerful People* is practical and valuable as a tool for praying and growing closer to the Lord in regular prayer. A beginner in the spiritual life could benefit immensely from this primer and old prayer warriors like myself can discover fresh insights into organizing one's daily prayer routine and living out of the joy of encounter with the living God. I love this small book and am delighted to recommend it. *The 5 Habits of Prayerful People* is going to be a hit with people seeking to deepen their relationship with God."

Rev. Wilfred J. Raymond, C.S.C.
President of Holy Cross Family Ministries

"The beauty of Mike St. Pierre's reflections is that they are based on his experience. St. Pierre's spot-on insights into practical engagement in prayer are clear, well written, and respectful of the awesome prayer tradition of our Church. *The 5 Habits of Prayerful People* has offered me new insights for my own life of prayer that I will make sure to share with others."

Rev. Michael T. Martin, O.F.M. Conv.
Director of Catholic campus ministry
Duke University

"*The 5 Habits of Prayerful People* provides many welcome and practical tips to finding God in the midst of our busy daily lives. Mike St. Pierre helps the reader cultivate time spent with God, time that actually yields deep dividends in every other area of our day. This book brings wisdom and insight into the challenges, the joys, and the rewards of personal prayer."

Rev. Michael White
Coauthor of *Rebuilt*

"Whether you're a prayer newbie seeking solace, a veteran spiritual soldier in search of a new tool, or simply a person of faith who deeply desires a more fruitful relationship with the divine, Mike St. Pierre's *The 5 Habits of Prayerful People* will be a gift for your daily walk with God. Full of practical tips and tools, this book reminds us that there is no one-size-fits-all system for grace.

It is the perfect companion to cultivate a prayer life that helps each of us answer the call to holiness in our own unique way."

Lisa M. Hendey
Founder of *CatholicMom.com* and author of *The Grace of Yes*

"Here is the witness of an incredibly busy administrator who has still found ways to make prayer and personal growth a priority in his life. With humility and humor, St. Pierre encourages each and every one of us to do the same. Busy people everywhere will find encouragement for building a habit of prayer in their lives."

Ann M. Garrido
Author of *Redeeming Administration* and *Redeeming Conflict*

"What if you could take the smartest tactics from everyday work and apply them to your faith? Mike St. Pierre's book does just that—it brings your daily productivity to your daily prayers."

Laura Stack
President and CEO of The Productivity Pro

"I loved this book! As someone who's constantly trying to excel at personal productivity, I learned in reading *The 5 Habits of Prayerful People* that it's not only about 'getting prayer done' but about taking my relationship with God to a whole new level. Mike St. Pierre shows how using good productivity habits can help make prayer an integral part of my daily life so that I can become a better follower of Christ."

Michael Sliwinski
Founder and CEO of Nozbe

"Instead of a textbook on prayer, we are offered a personal portrait of prayer. In *The 5 Habits of Prayerful People*, the reader is invited into Mike St. Pierre's decades-long journey of prayer—or, as Mike calls it, 'prayerfinding.' Much can be learned from a reflective reading of this work!"

Curtis Martin
Founder and CEO of FOCUS

THE 5 HABITS OF PRAYERFUL PEOPLE

A **NO-EXCUSES** GUIDE TO **STRENGTHENING** YOUR **RELATIONSHIP** WITH **GOD**

MICHAEL ST. PIERRE

AVE MARIA PRESS AVE Notre Dame, Indiana

Founded in 1865, Ave Maria Press is a ministry of the United States Province of Holy Cross.

www.avemariapress.com

Paperback: ISBN-13 978-1-59471-879-3

E-book: ISBN-13 978-1-59471-880-9

Cover image © DigitalVision.

Cover and text design by Samantha Watson.

Printed and bound in the United States of America.

Library of Congress Cataloging-in-Publication Data is available.

For Cary,
who has spent the better part of twenty years
reminding me that bigger things are always possible.

CONTENTS

FOREWORD

BY CHRIS LOWNEY

To write the foreword for his book on prayer, Mike St. Pierre wanted someone who models a robust, rewarding prayer life—a spiritual master who could share profound wisdom about prayer. Sorry, dear reader: I guess no such people were available, so you got me instead.

I'm joking, but I must admit that I'm not a spiritual guru who writes books about prayer. Rather, my ramshackle prayer life made me the target audience for Mike's book. So, come to think of it, maybe I'm the ideal person to write this foreword. Anything I write will be from the perspective of those of us who are not showered with mystical visions when we sit down to pray, in part because we don't sit down to pray nearly as often as we should! Before sitting down to write, though, I decided to inventory my prayer life. (By the way, that might not be a bad thing for you to do before diving into Mike's book.) Let me share some of my inventory, followed by some reflections on it.

I start almost every morning with a few minutes of prayer, done together with my wife. Our morning practice is rich and rewarding. Before each day's craziness begins, my wife and I remind ourselves why we're grateful, we share with the Lord (and each other) whatever concerns are on our mind, and we say the Lord's Prayer. We also read the day's gospel and a reflection on it. (Well, truth be told, we sometimes skip that part on days when my wife is cutting it so close that she has to run for the train.) In either case, after these few moments of morning prayer, I feel closer to the Lord and closer to my wife. I would call that a pretty good outcome.

And then? Well, I always carry a rosary ring in my pocket. (I'm sure you've seen them: a ring-sized circle of metal with ten protrusions and a small cross, enough to pray a decade of the Rosary.) If I'm walking to the train, or out for a casual walk, I often use that rosary ring to pray a decade (or two, or five, or even more). It puts me in a prayerful mood, and I stay with it until I start to get distracted. I've learned that the most important criterion of good personal prayer is whether it helps us grow closer to the Lord, not whether or not we're uttering lots of words with exquisite formulaic precision.

Do I pray consistently? Well, that's a very different story, which gets to another theme that runs through Mike's book. There are lots of things we all want to do to better our prayer lives, but there's often a huge gap between "I want to do this" and "let me schedule this for tomorrow, even though it means getting up fifteen minutes earlier or sacrificing ten minutes of social media scrolling." To his credit, Mike tackles the demands of our lives head on and makes lots of good suggestions as to how we might turn our aspirations into realities. He also provides clever ways we might use technology to help us.

I recently reviewed Pope Francis's exhortation on holiness, *Gaudete et Exsultate*. As one might suspect in a document on holiness, Francis talks a *lot* about prayer. What most struck me about the pope's discussion of prayer, however, was how often he mentions the word *listen*. My own prayer life involves me talking to God. But if a key purpose of prayer is to strengthen my relationship with God, I guess I should let the Lord do some of the talking too. Pope Francis recommends carving out time to be with God, to read scripture and discern in God's Word what he may be speaking to you at this moment in your life.

And that's a sweet spot of Mike's book. It's a book about prayer generally, but it's especially a book about getting better at the "listening" part of prayer. That's an area where most of us can use help. We all learned to talk, that is, to recite prayers. But most of us weren't really taught to listen. It feels uncomfortable and awkward. Remember how the prophet Elijah speaks of listening for God's "still, small voice"? The voice of God is easily drowned out by all the music, phone calls, television, and social media that distract me all day long. It can be hard to tune in to what the Lord may be saying. In *The 5 Habits of Prayerful People*, Mike gives lots of helpful advice on becoming better at tuning in.

Mike's book is a great place to start if you want to pray (or want to want to pray). He'll help you if you want to pray more (or more deeply). And if you've struggled before? Mike St. Pierre has the strategies and tools you need to establish a regular prayer life.

Happy reading! And even more, happy praying!

INTRODUCTION

I can still remember the day like it was yesterday. I was nineteen years old and a sophomore in college. My room was on the second floor of an underclassmen dormitory on the south side of campus at the Catholic University of America. Sitting in the standard hardback chair at the desk provided by the university, I had a set of rosary beads in one hand and a $1.99 booklet titled *How to Pray the Rosary* in the other hand. This book was the first one I found near the checkout line at the local Catholic bookstore. It was 8:00 p.m. With very little confidence and zero practice, I attempted to pray.

I wish I could say that it was a deeply contemplative and peaceful moment. It wasn't. Instead of an angelic look toward heaven, I was preoccupied with the sounds of floor mates outside my door. A radio played "Even Flow" by Pearl Jam. Someone was shaving in the bathroom with an electric razor, most likely not cleaning up after himself. Someone else was applying a cheap cologne to another student's doorknob. Let's be honest—cheap cologne on a doorknob is only rivaled by hiding someone's clothes when they've had too much to drink.

Ah . . . life as an undergrad!

Inside my room, I fumbled my way through the Rosary. It was hardly the experience I hoped it would be. For starters, I'm pretty sure I only prayed eight Hail Marys on the third decade. I found it darn near impossible to say the prayers *and* meditate on the Mysteries. Finally, it was unclear whether I was supposed to kiss the crucifix at the end or just make the Sign of the Cross while it was in my hand. Can we admit that there are a lot of mechanics when it comes to the Rosary? I feared that this first experience with the Rosary just might be my last. But I also wondered what was wrong with me: *Was I a loser? Seriously, wasn't praying the Rosary just part of the Catholic handbook? How could I, a cradle Catholic, not know how to pray?*

Don't get me wrong—I had *said* many prayers throughout my then nineteen-year life. What I hadn't done was spend time *in* prayer. Taking ten minutes on that night in 1993 felt like two hours in the car with someone I barely knew.

That experience and the questions it raised have followed me throughout my adult life. Perhaps you have had an experience like mine. Maybe you've asked these same questions too. Have *you* desired to be more prayerful but found you really didn't know how to pray? If so, this book is for you.

The answers to my questions about prayer arrived decades later, after I had spent considerable time and effort studying human productivity. The epiphany came through a conversation with Fr. Terry, a holy man whose "job" it is to give advice to people who desire to pray well. A priest friend had told me about Fr. Terry, and I set up an appointment. He struck me as quiet, intuitive, and introverted. We immediately hit it off. Fr. Terry is what is known as a spiritual director. He has been coaching me once every six weeks or so for years.

Fr. Terry once said this about prayer: "God waits for you there. Don't worry about the words or if you're doing it right. Just pray." These simple words, coupled with what I've learned about human productivity, have led me to form an approach to prayer that has changed my life.

Today, instead of worrying about the particular form of prayer, what to say or how to say it, I've focused on building up the *consistent habit* of prayer. Instead of chasing the latest spiritual fads, I've embraced the imperfect routine of showing up and simply trying my best to pray. These strategies have made all the difference.

When I decided to write a book about prayer, I realized that the process could be a lot like a middle-school science student attempting to write a thesis about astrophysics. What I've discovered, however, is that each one of us can write a book about prayer. The story God writes in each of us is worth telling.

Amazingly enough, we're all capable of praying well. Think about that for a second. You probably don't have the capacity to be a professional basketball player or a world-class cellist. You do, however, have the potential to become an expert in prayer. When you do something to develop that potential, you're taking steps toward becoming what Catholics call a saint. Now that's something we can all pursue. In fact, God calls every one of us to holiness.

Just as intriguing as my own spiritual journey has been the discovery that many others share the desire to pray. They struggle with prayer, as I have. I hear it through comments they leave on Facebook or send to me via email. They lack confidence at times and wonder if their prayers go unheard. They try to be prayerful, but then the busy pace of life swallows up their good intentions, pushing devotional time to the back burner.

Yet, I believe each of us has at least *some* desire to pray and pray *well*. The difficulty is that we lack what we need to build the muscle of prayer and, as a result, fall back into old habits.

Then we get stuck.

The good news is that *it doesn't have to be that way*. The tools people use to be productive in other endeavors can help. You really *can* become a person of prayer and learn to have confidence in our loving and merciful God. You *can* cultivate a habit of praying each day, even if you haven't been able to do so in the past. Even if you feel scattered or disorganized, you *can* become an expert in your own right. Your prayer *can* be fruitful and your relationship with God *can* be stronger.

How can you tell if you're on the right track? You know it when you notice yourself becoming more confident when you talk to God. When you listen to God, you have a concrete expectation that something is happening. When you pray for someone else, you're able to trust that you're heard and that God will respond in his time, the way he knows is best.

My ordinary experience in the fall of 1993 taught me something: The tiniest desire to pray can be enough to get you moving. That small seed is inside each of us, waiting to be watered and given light in order to grow. The water and light are provided by God. Our role is to show up and meet the God who waits for us in prayer.

As St. Teresa of Kolkata said, "Prayer is not asking. Prayer is putting oneself in the hands of God, at his disposition, and listening to his voice in the depths of our hearts."[1] In this way, prayer is nothing more than showing up and turning our hearts toward God.

We *can* apply to prayer the skills we've learned to be at our best in other aspects of our lives. All we have to do is acknowledge and affirm the desire to pray, and over time we'll learn how to pray well. We may not be the brightest students in the school of prayer, but we don't have to be because our teacher is God himself.

HOW TO USE THIS BOOK

In most schools, there are many doors. Having been the president of a Catholic high school, I can speak with some knowledge of this. At least once a year I would convene what was called "The School Safety Meeting" with my leadership team.

We would identify and lament the blind spots in our school's security: One back door was routinely left open by a coach. One first-floor closet never seemed to close. We joked about a coach who left the school years before and *supposedly* still had a key.

We would then make a series of resolutions aimed at making our school a little safer for the rest of the year. Usually these resolutions had something to do with Gustavo, our head of maintenance. An employee for more than twenty years, Gustavo had total knowledge of the building—he knew every leaky faucet, every crack in the sidewalk around the school. The man was, and still is, a walking encyclopedia of the facility. This included his vast collection of keys.

Gustavo's keys were like gold and his intimate knowledge of each key was legendary. A slight jig on one key meant something different from a minor jag on another key. Gustavo knew keys like a guitar player knows picks. It was almost as if Gustavo's keys were an extension of himself. Sometimes Gustavo wouldn't even look at a key. Simply by fingering the massive ring on his beltloop he knew which one opened each door.

One year a major emergency caused the entire administration more than a bit of angst: Gustavo lost his keys. Only when he found them, three days later, did we all breathe a sigh of relief. When you lose your keys, everything gets out of whack. This was certainly the case with Gustavo's keys.

Why all this talk about keys? Simply put, they open doors. So too does prayer. Prayer is often both a process of unlocking layers of intimacy and a result of daily habit. This book will examine five habits that are "keys" to prayer. I'll share each one with you, its intricacies and edges, so that you can better approach God through prayer. Some of these disciplines will require more of you, while others will become like muscle memory without much effort.

At the end of each chapter are a series of questions. You can answer these on your own or in a group. A section of my website is dedicated to helping you complete each chapter. You can find it at www.mikestpierre.com/prayer.

Don't take my word for it just yet. The saints have more to say about prayer than any other topic. Take St. Teresa of Avila as an example. She describes prayer as taking time frequently to be alone with the One we know loves us.[1] She came to understand prayer as a *process* rather than a point of perfection. Teresa's greatest work on prayer, *The Interior Castle*, was written toward the end of her life in 1577. To Teresa, the founder of her religious community and a companion of John of the Cross, prayer was nothing more than a journey inward. This path would lead one closer into union with Christ.

Any journey is scary, but when you're going inward, it can be downright terrifying.

In *The Interior Castle*, St. Teresa of Avila describes this journey of the soul as a castle with many rooms. Inside the castle are seven mansions, and each mansion contains many spaces. The outer rooms are associated with a person who is starting out in his or her faith. The closer one gets to the seventh mansion, the greater the level of intimacy with Christ. One enters the first mansion (as a creature of sin) and wanders all the way to the center of the castle, where one experiences the intimacy that awaits a bride of Christ. This is true connection.

Productivity experts talk about connection but in different terms. They describe being fully immersed in your work without any distractions between you and what you're doing. Often called *flow*, it's when you're fully present and totally engaged. When you're praying and sense that total connection to God, you're in a state of flow and that feels very good.

While I'm hardly a mystic, I have had moments of prayer when my body felt differently. At other times, it was as if time stood still and I could gaze at Christ on the Cross for what felt like hours.

You could easily misread *The Interior Castle* and presume that your faith is only going to get stronger. The spiritual life is not nearly as neat and clean as that, and it often includes regression and setbacks. Still, the concepts are useful to seeing spiritual growth as a series of steps.

When I first stumbled across *The Interior Castle*, I was immediately drawn into its central concept of *prayer as progress*. There are fits and starts, wins and losses. For St. Teresa of Avila, prayer is how to make the journey from the outer mansions to the very center of the castle. St. Teresa writes that we must have a "determined determination" to never give up on prayer.[2]

Can you relate to this? Are you determined to be determined to grow in prayer?

Your resolve to grow in prayer is very important. Like any habit, prayer is often one step forward and two steps back. I might spend twenty minutes in prayer on Monday and then forget to pray on Tuesday. I may then get back on the horse on Wednesday but face a setback on Thursday. This is how it goes.

St. Teresa wasn't the only one who taught that prayer is a series of steps. Pope John Paul II, who died in 2005 after having served as pope for more than twenty-six years, was also an adept professor of the mysteries of the interior life.

During his visit to the United States in 1987, Pope John Paul II addressed the young people gathered at the New Orleans Superdome. "Prayer is the key to the vitality of your life in Christ," he said, imploring them to pray. "Prayer is communion with God," he continued, "and it is prayer that makes us one with the Lord. Through prayer we come to share more deeply in God's life and in his love."[3]

Looking to the example of how Jesus prayed, the Holy Father noted the importance of both joy and perseverance related to prayer. It is when prayer is difficult that the believer must persevere most. Jesus' habit of prayer shows each of us that we must not stop praying in the face of fatigue or lack of knowledge. Pope John Paul II concluded his message with one enduring invitation, "And so, as long as the memory of this visit lasts, may it be recorded that I, John Paul II, came to America *to call you to Christ, to invite you to pray!*"[4]

Now that's a mission statement if there ever was one! The Holy Father travels to America and sums up his entire visit in one word—*pray*.

Pope John Paul II, like Teresa of Avila four centuries before him, knew that prayer was the key to growing in holiness. Prayer strengthens our relationship with the Lord.

As you can see, the ways of describing prayer are many. Thankfully, there's no one way to pray. There are, however, some common disciplines that unlock deeper intimacy with God.

Are you ready for greater intimacy with the Lord?

Let's begin.

PRAYER AND PRODUCTIVITY

It all started back in eighth grade. Instead of using one of those fancy homework notebooks, my preference was to take a simple 8½" x 11" sheet of paper and write down the day's assignments. On the left side of the paper was the list of courses; on the right the particular assignments. At the top of the page was the date and, if I remembered, a quote for the day. Each day, this nerdy ritual took on new forms. It eventually became what I was known for in my New England suburban school.

What I would realize years later is that this practice was the origin of my own interest in personal productivity. One sheet of paper, one day at a time. I had figured, although unknowingly at the time, that one simple sheet of paper would make my day run smoother. The page got me organized each day, and it formed a mobile system to keep me organized throughout the year. Eventually a couple of my buddies copied the system for their own use.

LIFE HACKING

In eighth grade I had learned my first lesson in what we now call "life hacking." *Life hack* can be defined as "a tip, trick, or efficient method for doing or managing a day-to-day task or activity."[1] In the eighth grade I was looking for the fastest way to keep all my tasks in one place. I still use a single sheet of paper this way today. I also still look for life hacks to apply to just about every area of my life.

I suspect engineers or scientists would be drawn to life hacks because of their fascination with how things work. For me, the draw is quite different. The fact is I'm *lazy*. That's why I'm always looking for faster and easier ways to get things done. I wish I had a more sophisticated or virtuous reason, but I don't. When I process the mail, I do it each Sunday and touch it once. When I do social media for work, I do it in one shot, scheduling an entire week of tweets and Facebook posts in less than an hour.

When I do yard work, I try to find the best way to mow my lawn in the least amount of time. These are all examples of life hacks. You probably have some too. Do you remember the last time that you put a sticky note on the back door as a reminder to do something? That's a life hack and a darned good one at that! There *are* faster, smarter, and better ways to do most everything. The more I read about productivity, the more I apply it to my daily work. Much of my online platform is dedicated to various strategies related to personal productivity and time management. I started a blog in 2008 to share these ideas with others. The posts range from tips on organizing your week to how to run a meeting. Since then, my blog posts have turned into podcasts and e-books, and the e-books have become online courses and even YouTube videos. The more I learn, the more I want to share with others.

I knew I was onto something when one of my employees brought in a special notebook for keeping his daily appointments. Another staffer read David Allen's *Getting Things Done*, a book almost on the level of the Holy Bible for life hackers. A third person suggested that we try a new productivity app so we could keep more organized. Something was catching on. Why? *There's something inside of us that makes us want to improve what we're doing or how we're doing it.*

KNOW YOURSELF

As time went on, I wanted to be even more productive. I decided that deeper self-knowledge would help me fine-tune my gifts and address my limitations. If there was a personality test, I took it and then told everyone I could about it. Myers-Briggs, DISC assessments, you name it—I had my entire leadership team participate.

The one assessment that resonated with me more than any other, however, was the one I was initially most skeptical of: the enneagram. The enneagram is a personality framework used by people from multiple faith traditions, based on nine numbered personality profiles. *The Enneagram: A Christian Perspective* by Fr. Richard Rohr, O.F.M., outlines how Christians can understand and apply the enneagram to everyday life in ways that are consistent with the truths of our faith.

As it turns out, I'm a type one, what the enneagram calls the Reformer. That is, I first see the goodness of the world and then the flaws evident throughout it. Ones are extremely self-critical perfectionists. It's said that you know that you're a one when you wake up in the morning and you hear a negative voice in your head. The voice rarely affirms and always critiques. My wife, Cary, once confronted me about this. She said, "Michael, you know what your problem is? You always want things to be better! Why can't you just be happy with life as it is?" She was calling out the *one*ness in me and she was right. (She's always right, but that's another book entirely!)

You see, ones live, breathe, and dream in lists. Because we want things to be perfect, lists allow us to categorize the improvements. A typical one probably has a framed quote from St. Augustine on their wall that reads, "Peace is the tranquility of order." (I know that I do.)

Learning more about myself has helped me make sense of my own list-making tendencies in light of my faith. It has also shown me my need to embrace the Lord and be a bit more compassionate toward myself. The idea of making lists might make you break into a cold sweat or run screaming to the nearest exit. But whatever your personality type is, it's what you bring to the table of everything you do. It's also what you bring to prayer. Learning more about your gifts and limitations helps you identify approaches that are likely to work, as well as those that aren't.

CHECKING THE BOX

As I continued to meet with Fr. Terry, my spiritual director, my life-hacking nerdiness and love for personality tests really kicked in. After some small talk, my smartphone would come out of my pocket and I would give my spiritual director a list of things I wanted to discuss. A journaling app made me even more arrogant. Each morning I'd read the daily Mass readings and then write down my thoughts and interpretations of them. My months became littered with daily entries, and when I would meet with Fr. Terry, I would show him my streak as if to say, "See right here—I'm on a roll! Fifty-three days in a row that I've been praying!" Not once did he laugh at me or tell me that it was usually the director who runs the show. Instead, he just listened.

Invariably Fr. Terry would tell me that prayer wasn't always about check boxes or measurable progress. I would nod and smile, but I had my doubts. What I really wanted to say was, "Yeah right, Fr. Terry. I'm hacking my way to heaven and you should too. Here's how you can download the app today!"

He *was* right, however. Intimacy with God is about *relationship*, not *measurement*. My prayer life was consistent. I attended Mass each Sunday and occasionally during the week. I participated in spiritual direction each month. I was even part of a faith-sharing group that met regularly. Still, while I could point to strings of daily prayer in my journal, it wasn't as if those entries represented much depth. Rather, they symbolized a check-in with the Lord. Not bad for a start, perhaps, but certainly not a moment of silent intimacy with the Almighty.

TAKE THE PLUNGE

My prayer lingered on the surface. I could only fake it so much when I visited with Fr. Terry. Of course, he knew that I was practicing a sort of spiritual "skimming." On one hand, I was relieved to accept his guidance. But on the other hand, I was frustrated that I wasn't growing faster. We both knew that there was a next chapter in my faith and in my prayer. What I didn't yet understand was that it wouldn't require a list at all.

So I took the plunge and did what was most uncomfortable. I decided to show up to a spiritual direction meeting without a list. That's right—no list at all. When Fr. Terry arrived in the room where we typically meet, the grin on my face alerted him that something was up. With no list or agenda to "cover" with my spiritual director, I was finally ready to receive whatever wisdom he had for me.

God had broken through. I realized that my desire to control, maintain order, and keep lists wasn't what I needed most. In the end, what I needed was to show up to prayer empty handed, ready to receive whatever God wanted to give.

LET GO

That day began a new stage in my spiritual life. Since then I have learned over and again the value of letting go. Lists are valuable, but sometimes they need to be left at the door. I began to see that God wanted me for himself, without a list in my hand or to-dos in my head.

Letting go is hard to do. I don't know about you, but I really like to be in control. My wife will tell you that I always start my day with a plan. My employees will tell you that I like to facilitate meetings because that way I get to decide how the meeting will go.

The desire for control can be unhealthy if left unchecked. Still, control gets a bad rap, just as with ambition and decisiveness. Control is part of life. Think of the last vacation you took—if you put together an itinerary, you were exercising some control. Or consider the last time you planned a party. If you made a list of decorations and food, you were asserting enough control over the situation to make you feel prepared. One weekend my kids wanted to go to a Mass later than the 9:00 a.m. service we usually attended. In a moment of self-control, I laid out our options in a list, making it easier to decide which Mass to attend. My exercise of control helped the family make a decision. But as a list keeper, I'm inclined to try to control every aspect of my life. I'm tempted to exercise control over *which* option is selected rather than just using my strengths to develop options for consideration by a group. This is when control becomes an issue and I need to turn it all over to the Lord.

To both surrender to God *and* maintain some semblance of (healthy) control, I needed to learn an entirely new way of being a Catholic Christian. Little did I know that God was about to show me a path that works for me and for others as well.

PRAYERFINDING

If I have learned anything from life hacks, it's that there's always a different way to do things. This applies to the spiritual life as much as anything else in life. The result is what I call *prayerfinding*. When you're a prayerfinder, you experiment. That is, you try and try again until you find what kind of prayer works best for you. How do you know when one style of prayer works better than another? The answer to this question varies, from how the experience makes you feel over time to whether it makes you a better person.

Most of us are not particularly good at trying new things with a goal in mind. Sure, we'll test out a new restaurant, but rarely will we give it a second shot if the food is less than stellar. We usually experience things in order to eliminate them. In contrast, we would do well to leave hasty judgments aside and learn to try new things with a spirit of resilience.

History is full of examples that illustrate this point. One I particularly like is that of Sir James Dyson, the inventor of the vacuum by the same name. By the time he introduced the Dual Cyclone cleaner in 1993, he had logged fifteen years and more than five thousand failed versions. When asked about whether his many failures were actually helpful, he said, "We have to embrace failure and almost get a kick out of it. Not in a perverse way, but in a problem-solving way. Life is a mountain of solvable problems and I enjoy that."[2]

Christians can find a way to do this when it comes to our prayer lives. It's just that most of us haven't been taught to practice the art of prayerfinding. To discover which methods and styles of prayer best suit our temperament takes time and grit. In fact, it can take years (and even decades) for a mature Christian to build spiritual momentum in prayer.

For me, prayerfinding has included exploring everything from charismatic prayer to the Rosary to centering prayer. With each experience I would ask three important questions:

1. *How do I feel after this experience?*
2. *In which ways did it bring me closer to the Lord?*
3. *Is this something I want to repeat on a regular basis?*

Here's what I learned in the process: I like charismatic prayer but have never considered myself a charismatic. When you're the only guy who doesn't pray in tongues, it's sort of like going to Yankee Stadium wearing a Red Sox jersey—*you feel out of place.*

As for the Rosary, I really *wanted* it to be part of my life. I still pray it occasionally and suspect that I'm going to learn to love it at some point. But try as I might, I can only pray the Rosary so often before it feels like a pair of shoes that just doesn't fit.

I continue prayerfinding. To some degree I'm still finding my way, tweaking and experimenting with various Catholic approaches to prayer. Can you relate? The bottom line: keep trying. Keep opening your heart to the Lord in all forms of prayer. The journey begins with a set of good habits, beginning with what I call the Habit of Passion and Pursuit.

Here are three steps to help you apply prayer and productivity to your life:

1. Download or print the Prayer and Productivity worksheet at www.mikestpierre.com/prayer.

2. Fill out the Prayer and Productivity worksheet, and answer the following three questions for yourself:

• Name an experience of prayer you considered enjoyable and/or fruitful. What was it that seemed to work well in that particular moment?
• Which day of the week do you find it easiest to pray? Why do you think that day stands out?
• If you could identify one area of your life (i.e., your job, hobbies, relationships) that needs more prayer, what would it be?

3. Pray: *Lord, help me to find you in prayer. As I reflect on the ways that you have already been present in my life, guide me toward a deeper relationship with you.*

THE 1ST HABIT

PASSION AND PURSUIT

Fr. Michael Martin is the director of campus ministry at Duke University. At six-foot-two and wearing his Conventual Franciscan habit, Fr. Mike has a larger-than-life presence. Beginning as freshmen and then throughout their time on campus, Duke students realize just how formidable Fr. Mike is as they get to know him. His homilies are thoughtful, his podcasts funny, and his extroverted personality is welcome in the midst of Duke's high-stress environment.

A few years ago I invited Fr. Mike to lead a team of school administrators in a day of recollection. As president of a Catholic high school here in New Jersey, I routinely brought in guests to lead our team in discussions of education, faith, and organizational excellence. Looking for the perfect speaker, I immediately thought of Fr. Mike. He didn't disappoint.

Fr. Mike said something to our team that I'll never forget: "If your faith is still at the level that it was when you received Confirmation, I feel bad for you." If I had ever said anything like that, it would have come across as condescending and my team would have been resentful. But sometimes a guest speaker can say those kinds of things without anyone taking offense. I suppose this is why consultants have a place in the world!

Fr. Mike's message didn't offend anyone. Rather, it resonated with all of us. In the days that followed, I couldn't help but ask myself whether *my faith* had grown since my Confirmation or whether maybe I was just getting older. *Was I really doing the work of discipleship, or was I just putting in the time?*

Doing the work, when it comes to our faith, has two parts: passion and execution. If you have passion but no plan, your spiritual life isn't likely to be much more than a flash in the pan. You might go from retreat to retreat or from one emotional experience to the next, but you probably won't be transformed.

On the flip side, if you have execution but no passion, you'll be really organized but lack soul. Attending Mass and developing other spiritual practices may become a series of check boxes, activities that are neat and tidy moving parts but empty. You'll lack the heart of an apostle and become a paper pusher rather than a missionary disciple in love with Jesus.

If Fr. Mike was visiting you, how would you respond to his words? Has *your* faith matured beyond when you were confirmed? The answers to this question lie beneath the 1st Habit for living a more prayerful life: the Habit of Passion and Pursuit.

PASSION

The word *passion* comes from the Latin word *passio*, meaning "to suffer." The word was introduced to Christianity in the earliest Latin translations of the Bible. It was typically associated with Christ's suffering and death on the Cross. In Catholic culture, a suffering Jesus is the centerpiece of religious artwork and imagery. Crucifixes with particularly bloody depictions of Christ became popular around the thirteenth century; in some parts of the world they're still the norm. Contrast this with the religious imagery of many other Christian traditions and it's clear—suffering holds a special place in the hearts of Catholics.

If you apply Christian teaching to the suffering we endure in everyday life, the narrative goes something like this: Jesus suffered and life is hard, so *offer it up*. When you do, you'll be uniting your suffering with the suffering of Jesus. That will make your suffering meaningful, and it will make you a better person.

Growing up, this unspoken message was one I ran away from. Give me a choice between camping or renting an RV and the choice is an easy one. I'll take the gas-guzzling RV every day of the week. (I mean, come on. Have you seen the size of the flat-screen TVs in those?) What about you? Are you drawn to or repelled by the Christian perspective on suffering? While stories of martyrdom are common even today, most Americans cringe when suffering is mentioned. It's simply inconvenient and unpleasant. It's *uncomfortable*.

Living in the most congested state in the nation, we New Jerseyans deal with pollution and traffic as if it's a badge of honor. Here, honking your horn at someone is a sign of respect. But Hurricane Sandy struck our hearts in 2013. For weeks, residents had no power. Gas lines were about a mile long, and I can remember driving to Pennsylvania just to fill up my tank. Those were tough days, and while we all pulled together, we became very aware of just how accustomed we are to Wi-Fi, Netflix, and a quick run to Starbucks. Hurricane Sandy reminded us that, even as gritty New Jerseyans, we'd become *soft*.

Maybe you've felt that way too. Think of the last time you had a cold. Did you wait it out or hurry to make a doctor's appointment so you could ask the physician to prescribe antibiotics? It's telling that often the first question a doctor asks is, "What's your pharmacy?"

SUFFERING OR SELF-FULFILLMENT?

Over the centuries our understanding of the word *passion* has changed radically. Today, *passion* no longer means "suffering" but rather "self-fulfillment." We're raised to "follow our passion," discover our "true passion," and live lives "full of passion."

While this has become our cultural mandate, it doesn't really resonate with most of us. I don't know about you, but my days are mostly filled with ordinary things. Wake up at 6:00 a.m. to take the dog out. Get in the car at 7:00 for the morning car pool. Report for work at 9:00. You get the point—daily life is fairly repetitive, uneventful, even boring. Our culture, however, persists in promoting passion as an end goal.

Rather than an element of suffering, passion is now crowned as the ultimate destination. Consider the cofounder of the most valuable company on the planet, Apple's Steve Jobs. His 2005 speech to the graduates at Stanford University tells you all you need to know about the current obsession with passion: "And most important, have the courage to follow your heart and intuition. . . . Everything else is secondary."[1]

This idea didn't originate with Jobs. It most likely started in 1970 with Richard Bolles, an Episcopal priest who was counseling distressed workers. Collecting some of his prior teachings on work-related advice, he wrote a 168-page book titled *What Color Is Your Parachute?* It became a best seller and spread the notion that happiness and work go together only if you "figure out what you like to do . . . and then find a place that needs people like you."[2] Today we think of this as run-of-the-mill good advice, but to audiences in the 1970s, it was revolutionary.

Two questions emerge: First, what impact does passion finding have on our spiritual lives? Second, is a passionate life attainable, or is pursuing it a waste of time?

To answer these questions, we can turn to one of the leading voices among those who counter the current "passion narrative," Georgetown professor Cal Newport. Newport eschews social media. If you email him, he will likely take weeks to get back to you (if he gets back to you at all). His 2016 book *Deep Work: Rules for Focused Success in a Distracted World* has become a favorite among life hackers.

Newport calls the obsession with finding one's deepest interest the *passion trap*. He describes it this way: "The more emphasis you place on finding work you love, the more unhappy you become when you don't love every minute of the work you have."[3]

Put another way, if you're always trying to find what's most interesting and enjoyable, you're likely to be let down. Newport's work has been bolstered by others such as Daniel H. Pink, a former speechwriter for Al Gore whose books on motivation have become best sellers. Pink argues that *purpose*, more than passion, is ultimately what motivates us: "We know that the richest experiences in our lives aren't when we're clamoring for validation from others, but when we're listening to our own voice—doing something that matters, doing it well, and doing it in the service of a cause larger than ourselves."[4]

For Pink, Newport, and others, the exhausting quest for a passionate life isn't all it's cracked up to be. A purpose-filled life, on the other hand, is more than it may appear to be.

THIRST FOR GOD

Now before you throw passion out the window, hold your horses. Passion as it relates to prayer might actually be a good thing. Let me show you what I mean.

Passion, when it's rightly employed, can be a powerful asset in the spiritual life. It might also be described as zeal or thirst. The scriptures are full of passages that help us understand how passion can be integrated into our faith. Psalm 42:2–3 captures this beautifully:

> As the deer longs for streams of water,
> so my soul longs for you, O God.
> My soul thirsts for God, the living God.
> When can I enter and see the face of God?

Again, in Psalm 63:2:

> O God, you are my God—
> it is you I seek!
> For you my body yearns;
> for you my soul thirsts,
> In a land parched, lifeless,
> and without water.

These Old Testament themes are, not surprisingly, complemented by New Testament passages. In John 4, Jesus has a conversation, perhaps the longest recorded conversation in his ministry, with a Samaritan woman. The "woman at the well" is curious about what Jesus can offer her. His reply is telling: "'Everyone who drinks this water will be thirsty again; but whoever drinks the water I shall give will never thirst; the water I shall give will become in him a spring of water welling up to eternal life.' The woman said to him, 'Sir, give me this water, so that I may not be thirsty or have to keep coming here to draw water'" (vv. 13–15).

The lives of the saints give us concrete examples of those who had what we might call a passionate relationship with the Lord. In the fourth century, St. Augustine taught extensively about the interchange between humanity and God. To him, the highway of prayer formed when God's passion and ours meet. "Whether we realize it or not, prayer is the encounter of God's thirst with ours. God thirsts that we may thirst for him."[5]

You may be more familiar with St. Augustine's famous words: "You made us for yourself, O Lord; our hearts are restless until they rest in you."[6]

In the fourteenth century, St. Catherine of Siena takes it further: "If you would make progress, then, you must be thirsty, because only those who are thirsty are called: 'Let anyone who is thirsty come to me and drink.'"[7] In St. Catherine's mystical writing, *The Dialogue*, she explains further that a passion for God isn't only desirable but also necessary: "Those who are not thirsty will never persevere in their journey."[8] When life gets tough, it's the enduring passion for God that helps us see the forest through the trees. As our busy lives make prayer seem unattainable, this thirst for God is all the more necessary.

My own prayer journey has reflected this. There have been times in which prayer has been accompanied by great waves of emotion and other times in which prayer hasn't "felt" like much of anything at all. A growing passion for God was the constant.

A PLACE FOR PASSION

In my life, the depth of prayer became tangible in college. When I wasn't applying cheap cologne to the doorknobs of my roommates, I was getting to know a place called Caldwell Chapel. It is said that Archbishop Fulton J. Sheen used to pray for hours at a time in this chapel, and while it may not be on the official campus tour, it became a hot spot for me in those years of young adulthood.

Each day, as classes ended and people retreated to their dorms to study, I would make my way to Caldwell Chapel. Most days, I would read my Bible and journal. It was there, too, that I first discovered Thomas Merton, St. Augustine, and Sheen. I learned that I could sit with the Lord for long periods of time. While some days were a chore, more often than not I found the hour to be doable. Every so often, it was as if God just drew me in and pulled me closer to himself. *Simply amazing.*

Looking back on this, now that life is much fuller and busier with four kids at home, I have fond memories of the hours spent at Caldwell Chapel. It was in the chapel that I can say I felt God's presence. Sometimes my face would grow warm. At other times I could sit for long stretches gazing at the crucifix. This was a season of *feeling* and real learning. My heart and mind were stretching toward God—I was thirsty.

BEYOND FEELINGS

Perhaps you have had a similar season of prayer in your life. Or maybe that kind of experience is yet to come. As often happens, however, this season came to an abrupt end when I graduated and headed off into "the real world." Prayer became more difficult and quite sporadic. It's not that I didn't have the time. Rather, I lacked the feelings that had so often accompanied my prayers during college. I was experiencing what is often called "spiritual dryness." For better or worse, it lasted for several years. I dare to say that this is quite common among believers.

Now in my forties, I think that period of dryness *was* a good thing. St. Francis de Sales advised that in prayer we must not seek the consolations of God but the God of consolations.[9] It's easy to be passionate about prayer when it feels good or when life is going smoothly. The point is to maintain a passion for God even when life is difficult. The seasons of spiritual dryness are very similar to those that occur with your best friend or your spouse. It's not always roses. The discipline is to keep showing up. (We'll take a closer look at that in the next chapter.) Who knew that something as intense as passion could be practiced as a discipline?

Showing up requires a healthy dose of passion, not just the feeling but also the longing. Sometimes prayer will feel warm and breezy, and other times, dry as a bone. Dos Equis ads aside, the key is to stay thirsty for God.

Christopher West is considered to be the most recognized teacher of St. John Paul II's Theology of the Body. One of West's most common themes? The "ache of the heart." In a recent review of a popular movie, West put it this way: "We're often afraid to feel that deep 'ache' of our hearts because we intuit that to feel it is to lose control of our nice, orderly lives. Yes, that is correct. In Christian terms, it's called surrender or abandonment to God. Those who have the courage to feel the abyss of longing in their souls and in their bodies and open it up in complete abandonment to the One who put it there will, indeed, have 'messy' lives . . . but messy in a beautifully hopeful way."[10]

As it turns out, the ache, our hunger and thirst for God, constitutes the passion that propels us deeper in prayer.

This leads to the second half of the 1st Habit—*pursuit*.

PURSUIT

When I first discussed the idea of this book with my wife, Cary, she found the word *pursuit* to be odd. "It feels kind of masculine, like you're trying to accomplish something. Sometimes it's enough just to be yourself before God." I thought, *Why does this woman have to be right all the time?*

Still, passion without execution isn't fruitful.

That's where the idea of pursuit comes in. With respect to prayer, I define *pursuit* as "striving toward God in a thoughtful way." We've already discussed the ache for God. Pursuit is the other side of the coin—*a thoughtful way* to turn the ache into action. That's the *striving* part.

After all, if you just pine for someone and don't tell the person you love them or never invite them to spend time with you, your ache will be for nothing. Likewise, if you just think about God and never try to *live* like God or spend time with him, your effort will only go so far. It's here that James's epistle rings true: "Do not merely listen to the word, and so deceive yourselves. Do what it says. Anyone who listens to the word but does not do what it says is like someone who looks at his face in a mirror and, after looking at himself, goes away and immediately forgets what he looks like" (1:22–24, NIV).

ACTION

Real holiness always flows from intent *and* action; belief *and* behavior. You and I already know this. What we may lack is a consistent teaching to guide us, one that tells us *how* to put our faith into action. The Habit of Passion and Pursuit is ultimately about giving form to the desire each of us has to become holy, to live as sons and daughters of God.

INTENT

Think about it—when you're thoughtful about something, you're more likely to do it well. You're intentional. This applies to almost everything—the last dinner you cooked, the last time you mowed your lawn, the last birthday gift you bought. When we have a goal, and then plan to work toward it, things always go better. When you go into a grocery store and you have a list, you're more likely to get what you need and want (and less likely to wander the aisles gathering a cartful of random items). Each one of us is a "project manager" in this regard.

But what about our prayer lives? Is it okay to look at prayer as a *project* that can be tackled with purpose? Yes and no.

"PROJECT PRAYER"

Prayer, however, is about relationship, so it's not the same as other "projects" you might have in your life.

Consider something simple such as cleaning out your garage. You have an end goal: a clean, orderly garage that is used as a place for your car, tools, and more. As a project, it has a starting point—let's say this Saturday. You know exactly what you'll need to accomplish the job: trash bags, a broom, time, and, of course, the will to undertake the work. Give it enough time and your garage will be clean. This kind of project is very satisfying, and you can easily cross it off your list. It's simple.

Other projects are more complicated. In the to-do app on my smartphone I have a project for work called "Recruit New Board Members." Unfortunately this isn't as simple as cleaning my garage. To complete this task, which actually doesn't have an end date, I need to find talented individuals to join our board at work. To make it more complicated, I need to collaborate with other selection committee members assigned to this project. I need them to help me. Then, once we find good candidates, we have to interview and vet each individual. Finally, we need the existing board to then vote on our recommendations. It's quite a process! And because the selection committee and the candidates change every year, it's a moving target that requires a deft hand at the wheel.

Your relationship with God has some similarities. You know the end goal: intimacy with Jesus Christ. You acknowledge that you have to put your heart (passion) into it. You know that it will take some time. You also know that you'll never fully accomplish your goal until you reach heaven. To top it off, you also know that *you* are not the "project manager."

NOT ONE MORE THING

Let me be perfectly clear: *your relationship with God isn't one more thing to put on your to-do list.* The power of the Holy Spirit, wooing us closer into the heart of the Trinity and into a passionate love affair with God himself, is more mysterious than we can ever grasp. But—hear me out—I propose that investing a bit more work in our prayer lives might serve us some good.

You see, we don't have a crisis today in the Church in terms of doctrine—the truth is all there for the taking. Rather, we have a "how-to" crisis in terms of prayer and discipleship. Think of the last five homilies you heard. (You were listening, right?) Now, think of the practical suggestions that the deacon or priest offered in terms of putting your faith into action. I'm guessing your list is pretty thin. I know that mine is.

You and I know that God loves us and wants our lives to invite others into relationship with him. It's *how to do this* that's difficult, which is why the second half of the 1st Habit, pursuit, is so important.

STEP BY STEP

Pursuit is about breaking down something into doable, measurable steps. It may be the most difficult discipline of all. When you add pursuit to your prayer life, you're telling the Lord that you're serious about your relationship with him, that it means something to you. You're telling God that you're stepping up and doing your part. You're going beyond words and into action.

Let me share the opposite of what I mean. For years, I thought I was keeping my upper body in good shape. I would do thirty pushups a night and an occasional set of barbell curls. One day I saw a photo of myself from a trip we took to Cape Cod. There was my beautiful wife, walking on the beach. Next to her was a man with a slightly round middle. That man was me. To make matters worse, my incredibly chiseled biceps and chest muscles were not as defined as I had thought. I had unknowingly developed a "dad bod." Shocking, but true.

When I took an honest look at myself, I realized that I wasn't as defined as I thought. In fact, my family pointed out (as my kids like to do) that I was getting a little flabby. I had thought that my thirty pushups per night were enough. What I had underestimated was the force of turning forty and the lack of exercise. The result was a body that made me cringe. I wasn't fat, but unless I changed what I was doing, a chiseled beach body was going to be nothing more than a pipe dream.

I wasn't really *pursuing* fitness. I was flirting with it on a regular but shallow basis. I had the intent of being physically fit but I lacked the intentional plan for how to be as strong as I desired to be.

Are you doing this same thing with God?

Is your prayer life a tease with the Almighty? Do you feel as if each conversation you have with God amounts to mere small talk? If so, I suggest taking the first step in your pursuit of God. Don't wait another day to put your faith-filled intentions into action.

WHERE ARE YOU WITH JESUS?

A first step in bringing more pursuit to your prayer is to acknowledge where you are. As you're reading this book, where are you in your relationship with Jesus Christ? I find one section from the description of the Passion, in Mark 14:43–52, to be especially helpful in answering this question:

> Just as he was speaking, Judas, one of the Twelve, appeared. With him was a crowd armed with swords and clubs, sent from the chief priests, the teachers of the law, and the elders. Now the betrayer had arranged a signal with them: "The one I kiss is the man; arrest him and lead him away under guard." Going at once to Jesus, Judas said, "Rabbi!" and

kissed him. The men seized Jesus and arrested him.
Then one of those standing near drew his sword and
struck the servant of the high priest, cutting off his
ear. "Am I leading a rebellion," said Jesus, "that you
have come out with swords and clubs to capture me?
Every day I was with you, teaching in the temple
courts, and you did not arrest me. But the Scriptures
must be fulfilled." Then everyone deserted him and
fled. A young man, wearing nothing but a linen garment, was following Jesus. When they seized him, he
fled naked, leaving his garment behind. (NIV)

Through Mark's Passion narrative, we see that Jesus was
abandoned by many of the followers who were closest to him.
Three individuals in the above passage are especially worth
mention:

The disciple who cuts off the servant's ear. While Mark isn't clear
that this is Peter, this disciple clearly has passion and responds
accordingly. His faithfulness to Christ manifests in his emotional
response to the arrest of Jesus.

The disciple who betrays. Poor Judas, forever known as the
betrayer. Sometimes we forget that Judas was chosen by Jesus
to be a disciple. John's gospel says that Jesus knew of Judas's
plans and chose him anyway. Judas's faithfulness to Christ gets
derailed when the lures of the world pull him away. Whether
it was the money itself or something in Judas that longed for
greater recognition, he lost his way.

The disciple who flees naked. Perhaps one of the most over-
looked individuals in the gospels, this mystery man was at the
scene of Jesus' arrest wearing only a linen cloth. Some Bible
scholars think that this was Mark himself. (The scene reminds
me of every Marvel movie in which Stan Lee makes a cameo,
disguised as someone else.) Others believe it was Joseph of Ari-
mathea who would later wrap Jesus' dead body in a linen cloth,
adding to the symbolism of the cloth. Whoever this man was,
his brief appearance in this passage is certainly curious.

Have you ever felt like the disciple who had an emotional response to Jesus? While you may not have cut off someone's ear—now that would be a visual!—you may be a person who is prone to highs and lows. Maybe you've gone on a retreat and received the gift of tears. Maybe your prayer is often marked by deep feelings of God's presence.

Now look at Judas. While I would never want to be on the same softball team as Judas, if I'm honest, I've betrayed Jesus many times. When I make an idol out of something, I'm leaving Jesus behind in my pursuit of something else, something newer and shinier. I'm not afraid to tell you that I've confessed the sin of idolatry in the Sacrament of Reconciliation. Technology and material things challenge me. Each time some new gadget is introduced, I have to fight the urge to go and buy it. How about you? Which vice are you wrestling with? What pulls at your heart?

Last but not least, we get to the naked man fleeing the scene. (Don't worry, I'm not going to launch into a paragraph about nude discipleship.) All we have is a line about a man who followed Jesus faithfully but then becomes so frightened that he leaves with nothing on. In that moment he would rather be seen naked than stay close to Jesus and have others know who he was. An amazing scene! Would you prefer to follow Jesus in the dark? Would you rather be seen as a fan, watching from a distance, than as a disciple sharing Jesus' fate?

We can find ourselves in each of these three disciples: the emotional man with the sword, the one who betrays, and the frightened disciple who flees. I can describe the seasons of my faith when I genuinely felt the presence of God. I can also share—I'm not proud to admit it—that I've betrayed Jesus for far less than a bag of silver. Finally, I can relate to the man who would rather worship Jesus in anonymity than be known as a disciple in public. What about you?

TAKE INVENTORY

To help you with your own faith inventory, try the following strategy. Carve out time for yourself. Choose a time that won't conflict with anything else on your calendar. If you're a parent at home with the kids, wait until they're at school and then find a quiet block of time. If you have a commute, use that time for prayer. By making "time for yourself," you'll really be making time for the Lord.

Here are three steps to help you apply the Habit of Passion and Pursuit to your life:

1. Download or print the 1st Habit worksheet at www.mikestpierre.com/prayer.
2. Fill out the Habit of Passion and Pursuit worksheet, and spend five minutes alone reflecting on this quote from St. Thérèse of Lisieux: "For me, prayer is a surge of the heart; it is a simple look turned toward heaven, it is a cry of recognition and of love, embracing both trial and joy."[11]
3. Consider the following questions: What is one area of your life where you've been spinning your wheels, without visible results? What's one thing you can do this week to take action?

THE 2ND HABIT
PRESENCE

With the 2nd Habit, we start to get very practical about our prayer lives. Having grasped the importance of passion and pursuit, we look to *presence*.

Here, it's all about showing up.

This concept may seem like common sense, and that's because it is. The problem, though, is that it's never been more difficult to be present than it is right now. As you're reading this, email is flooding your in-box and your phone is likely buzzing with incoming text messages. It's not easy to show up to each moment of our day. That's why I'd like to tell you about Christine O'Brien.

Christine is the mother of five children, and she and her husband, Kevin, have lived in Pennsylvania for the greater part of their marriage of nearly twenty years. Originally from New Jersey, Christine was raised in a large family. She and Kevin met as classmates in the local Catholic elementary school.

Christine is passionate about life and lives with a sort of exuberance that is contagious. Having known her since my early twenties, I have always found Christine to be a good friend, the kind you want when life gets hard. She often texts out of the blue to let you know that she's praying for you or that she wants you to come over for dinner. Her life is lived with purpose. When she tells her children to clean their rooms, they do so. Her morning routine has a particular purpose: to get the kids out the door in as little time as possible. She sends out New Year's cards instead of Christmas cards because she doesn't want her family update to get lost in the postal buildup around December 25. Christine does *everything* for a reason.

Her prayer life is no exception. Christine, a lifelong Catholic, is one of the most prayerful women I know. When her kids were younger and time was scarce, she described prayer like this: "Prayer is like a loaf of bread. Some days, you get all of the slices and other days, just a piece or two. On a very hectic day with the kids, I may get just a few crumbs. If I'm attentive, these crumbs can add up to a full loaf."

Now that's wisdom from a woman who knows a thing or two about prayer.

You see, what I didn't mention is that Christine's life has been anything but easy. When a near-fatal car accident in her twenties forced her into months of physical therapy, she turned to God in prayer. When cancer took the life of her second-oldest daughter, Catie, again Christine turned to God in prayer. When her father faced years of debilitating illness—you guessed it— she turned to God in prayer. Christine's prayer life isn't on the surface. Rather, it's lived in the deep waters of uncertainty and trust. When Christine prays, she knows that God listens. That's because when Christine prays, *she's* listening to God. She has learned how to be in the moment because she realizes that God is fully present wherever she finds herself.

THE MYSTERY OF HERE AND NOW

Showing up and being present are much harder than they sound. The award for perfect attendance in school gets overshadowed by the highest GPA and the most championship medals. Still, it matters an awful lot.

One saint who practiced the Habit of Presence particularly well was St. John of the Cross. This sixteenth-century Carmelite was described by St. Teresa of Avila as the "father of my soul." Let that sink in for a minute. St. Teresa is describing another saint, one considerably younger than she was, as her spiritual mentor. This is a man we can *all* learn from.

Having joined the Carmelites as a young man, John desired to leave the order to enter the Carthusians so that he could dedicate more of his day to prayer. He loved silence and felt that a strictly cloistered Carthusian vocation would provide more time for quiet. Before leaving the Carmelites, however, he met Teresa of Avila. She persuaded him to reconsider, and instead recruited him to help her renew the Carmelite order.

The reform of the Carmelites proved quite difficult. John was seen as a threat to his own religious brothers and found himself in conflict with his own community. At the age of thirty-five, he was jailed, humiliated, and tortured for nearly a year. With only a window set high on the wall and the sound of nature outside, John was reduced to nothing. With no earthly comfort and hardly a hope for escape, John could do nothing *other than pray*. It was during this time that John first experienced the "dark night of the soul," an extended and intense period of spiritual dryness.

He described the dark night like this: "to the spirit, it does so only to give it light in everything; and that, although it humbles it and makes it miserable, it does so only to exalt it and to raise it up."[1]

Nine months later, John managed to escape through a small window. His vocation and ministry flourished, and his writings became a source of encouragement for those who struggle with prayer. He wasn't an academic. He didn't have a weekly column in a popular magazine. He wasn't first in his class. The man simply prayed. He showed up to the moment in which he found himself.

That simplicity paid off for John. His faithfulness to the daily task of prayer provided the context for God's grace to break through. John needed the dark night in order to find the day. Today the Church regards him as one of the greatest mystics in all of history.

FIVE CORE PRACTICES

John of the Cross had Teresa of Avila as a companion. He was a Carmelite priest with years of theological training. The average Catholic simply doesn't have these advantages. (Of course, most of us aren't being held captive in a closet either.) Still, how are we supposed to find the light?

Even worse, the increasing secularization of our culture has taken its toll. Fewer Catholics see God as central to their lives, and many Catholics feel distant from God. They may not go to Mass on Sundays. They don't have a regular time of daily prayer. When struggles come, they lack real confidence in God.

Here's what writing and teaching about prayer for more than a decade have taught me: cultivating a habit of prayer isn't half the battle—it's *all* of it. Often described as a muscle, prayer takes practice. In other words, you've got to do your part of the work and leave God to do his part. I see five core practices when it comes to the Habit of Presence:

1. **Willpower.** When it comes to prayer, willpower just isn't enough. We get tired. Life gets busy. We forget. Still, making use of whatever willpower we have can help us. As the day goes on, my willpower tends to decrease as my body loses its energy. While there are exceptions to this rule, prayer time should occur when we have the most willpower. For me, that's the morning.

2. **Regular Time.** Almost everyone who prays does so at a regular time each day. It's valuable to take some time to consider which part of the day allows you to get difficult things done. Is it in the morning? Is midafternoon a good time for you to tackle complex tasks? Or are you at your best in the evening? For many of us, the morning is the time of day when our willpower is strongest and our resistance is weakest. We're trying to cultivate a habit of praying and that's why a regular daily time of prayer is so important. This doesn't exclude spontaneous moments of prayer but grounds those moments in a daily check-in with God.

3. **Tools.** People who undertake something in an intentional way need to have the right tools for the job. Just like laying out your work clothes the night before, it makes sense to lay out your "prayer tools" as well. By this I mean your Bible, a journal, spiritual reading, rosary beads, and the like. If you have to work hard just to locate your Bible, chances are you

won't end up praying. Put your tools in a place you'll find them without having to expend any of your willpower.

4. **Silence.** We're used to living in a very noisy and sound-saturated world. As a result, most of us feel uncomfortable with the silence we encounter in an elevator or car. That discomfort is heightened in our relationship with God. When it comes to prayer, silence is difficult, especially at first. *Why isn't God saying anything? How long should I sit like this in silence?* These questions are normal and will decrease with time and practice.

5. **Tracking.** Measurement is part of almost everything we're serious about. Fitness gurus monitor their heart rate, diabetics watch their blood glucose, and a person who prays does well to track their prayer. This might be in the form of a journal entry, a calendar, or even an app that records the days you've prayed. This practice seems counterintuitive, and I can hear you saying, "You want me to track my prayer?" Absolutely, at least as you get started. Once you become accustomed to daily prayer, you'll need it less.

MORE WINS

As I said, showing up in prayer also has the potential to positively influence other parts of your life. In productivity terms, the Habit of Presence is aligned with what's often called "full engagement." That's the notion that when I'm practicing the art of being fully present, I can better serve those around me. How can we be *fully* present? We stop multitasking and focus attention only on what's in front of us. We choose not to be distracted and stop wishing we were somewhere else, doing something else. We're "all in" with whatever is right there in front of us.

Evangelical missionary Jim Elliot once said, "Wherever you are, be all there." The Habit of Presence allows you to give God the time he deserves (and you need) through your prayer life.

This brings order to other areas of your life, including work, home, friendships, and family relationships.

When you're fully engaged, you're honoring God's presence in the present moment and making yourself accessible to him. It's a mind-set of "being here" as opposed to somewhere else.

AT HOME

If you're always looking somewhere *else*, you're likely to miss what's right under your nose. My daughter recently explained to me the concept of FOMO, or the "fear of missing out." FOMO can cause us to be overly concerned with what others are doing. The explosion of tweets and Facebook and Instagram posts can make us feel less attractive, less intelligent, and downright boring. When we're feeling a lot of *less*, we're not growing in confidence.

I know when I scan my own Instagram feed, I see perfectly sculpted abs and toned biceps. I see pristine living rooms and vacations that are out of this world. I see a lot of *perfect*, and while I'm pretty good, I just don't stack up very well against perfection.

Many people experience FOMO and then regret that they aren't more interesting, athletic, or adventurous. It isn't a bad thing to want more from life. What's dangerous about FOMO is that most of what's posted online isn't real.

Let me give you an example of how FOMO can impact your spiritual life and alleviating FOMO moments can help you build the Habit of Presence.

You may not know that when celebrity Instagram posts are sponsored by a company, the celebrity earns money for each sponsored post. Topping the list in 2017 was Selena Gomez. One sponsored post from Gomez to her 123 million followers earned nearly half a million dollars.[2] Let that sink in for a minute—*one post earned Gomez half a million dollars.* You and I are in the wrong business!

In 2017, travel bloggers Lauren Bullen and Jack Morris revealed how much time they put into editing the photos they post on Instagram. Each photo is tweaked, modified, and edited to achieve social media perfection.[3] So much for taking a picture of a spontaneous moment and then posting it online! What's a Christian response to this? While you could quit social media cold turkey, another approach might be to step back and cherish the life you have, warts and all.

Think about this very moment right now—you have intellect and curiosity enough to read this book. You have a desire to grow in prayer. You already have a life worth living, even if Selena Gomez has more Instagram followers than you do.

In 2013, Chip and Joanna Gaines made their debut on HGTV through their show *Fixer Upper*. For five years they dazzled viewers with a combination of charm, humor, and an eye for home design. A typical episode provided a couple with several homes in need of renovation to choose from and a budget with which to do the work. The results were stunning: sparkling new kitchens, luxurious bathrooms, and an overall renovation that every home owner would envy.

Amy Anderson of *Success* magazine sums up the Gaines's appeal this way: "Their likability is the key to the show's success. His goofiness and her comedic timing pair well with the authenticity they present."[4] Five years after the debut of *Fixer Upper*, the couple announced that their hit show would be coming to an end. After seventy-nine episodes, they were ready to focus on other endeavors.

If *Fixer Upper* taught viewers anything, it's that an eye for what looks nice plus knowing how to get the most out of your money can make for a beautiful home. HGTV has used shows such as *Fixer Upper* and others to bring the home design business to an entirely new level. HGTV has helped people either love their current home or long for something else.

Discontent

One drawback to HGTV and shows such as *Fixer Upper* is that they can leave us feeling as if our own homes are terrible. Imagine a steady diet of *Fixer Upper* and you're likely to dislike the couch you're sitting on. But what if instead of longing for another home in another neighborhood in another state, you could be content with the home you have? This, of course, applies to much more than just the home you live in. There's a spiritual truth here as well.

In *Love the Home You Have: Simple Ways to . . . Embrace Your Style, Get Organized, Delight in Where You Are*, author Melissa Michaels explains that the dream home you see on TV might be right under your nose. Instead of wishing you were somewhere else, you could embrace the space that God has already given you. Michaels writes, "You and I can both discover contentment in the same place and at the same time. That would be right here, right now."[5]

I'm not saying that you shouldn't binge-watch *Fixer Upper* but rather that your home, daily schedule, and to-do list are where you're meant to be. What you have is what you should focus on. That's what being present looks like. Rather than wanting to be somewhere else, what if you could embrace God's presence in the midst of your ordinary life? This right-here-right-now approach to life is what the Habit of Presence is all about.

AT WORK

When it comes to work, being present is harder than it's ever been. When I became a remote worker leading a nonprofit, I was able to work from home. The unlimited supply of coffee and the ability to take a brief nap or run an errand after lunch was enough for me to say "sold!" But working remotely has its drawbacks too. It isn't always easy to connect with coworkers in a way that communicates care and understanding. They can feel as if I'm remote not only physically but also emotionally.

Most of us, however, don't work from home. The typical workplace is full of interruptions, bad lighting, and lousy meetings. Tack on a commute and an occasional annoying coworker and work can be a tough pill to swallow. A 2017 study found that 51 percent of American workers feel disengaged at work,[6] while another 2017 survey of seventeen thousand workers found that 71 percent were either "actively looking for new job opportunities" or had the idea of doing so on their minds "always, often, or sometimes."[7]

Seven Strategies for Work

It's difficult to be fully present at work, but it doesn't have to be that way. Having supervised hundreds of employees over many years, I've developed a few strategies for being more present (and therefore happier) at work:

1. **Routines cut down on stress.** To the degree that you can routinize your day, your productivity and general peace of mind will increase. Find a way to build a morning routine that works for you every day instead of having to stress each morning.
2. **Focus on what you can control.** One hundred percent of bosses are flawed. By focusing on what you can control about your work rather than the ways in which your supervisor or coworkers are imperfect, you'll be much happier.
3. **Name your next step.** Most people who are unhappy at work feel trapped. They often complain or push back, which can put them at risk for being fired. Before you quit or get fired, take the time to reflect. What would you like to do next? Is there a company that you would love to work for? Is there a particular role you'd like to play?
4. **Consider your context.** I once worked with a man who had worked in only one school for more than thirty years. He

was cranky and mean. No one knows what he would have been like if he had found a different job in a different school, but I suspect he would have been happier. You should probably consider changing your workplace every seven to nine years.

5. **Keep a "smile file."** I've done this for years and it works like a charm. When someone sends you a note, email, or message expressing gratitude, put it in a file. Receive a good performance review? Put that in the file. Once a year, take five minutes to look at your file. I promise it will put a smile on your face!

6. **Get some perspective.** Do you have a mentor or spiritual director you can talk to about your job? An outside perspective can often validate, challenge, or affirm your role at work. Just having someone to talk to makes a big difference.

7. **Begin a gratitude journal.** Research suggests that keeping a gratitude journal can improve your overall outlook on work.[8] I do this in my morning devotional time by listing at least five things that I'm thankful for from the past day. What are you thankful for?

These seven strategies can help you be more present at work. They can also connect to your life of prayer. As you cultivate a "being here" mind-set during your nine-to-five life, you'll be more likely to connect your job to your reason for working in the first place. Embracing what's right in front of you is part of what it means to "find God in all things," to quote the Jesuit maxim.

FOCUS

We've considered the Habit of Presence as it relates to both home and work. How might this concept show up in something as basic as your ability to focus?

The name Shawn Blanc probably doesn't mean anything to you. He doesn't have as many Instagram followers as Selena Gomez (or Joanna Gaines for that matter). He doesn't do Facebook, and if you were to see him at the grocery store, you probably wouldn't notice him.

Shawn, to his credit, has built a multimedia empire without a care for who recognizes him in the supermarket. His websites the Sweet Setup, Tools & Toys, and the Focus Course all provide Shawn with ways to teach his visitors about the ability to focus.

The Focus Course in particular is made up of forty-seven videos, downloadable worksheets, and online discussions. Shawn describes focus as "a skill you can learn (and continually improve). You will walk away with the ability to focus on the areas of life that matter most to you, while still maintaining a healthy balance in the others."[9]

The Habit of Presence is intrinsically related to your ability to focus. Shawn knows this and has built his entire professional success on this skill. He has seen it produce dramatic results in his work and in his life.

POSITIVE SIDE EFFECTS

As you put the 2nd Habit into practice, you'll notice that your ability to pray improves your ability to focus at other spots in the day. It's almost like taking a medicine with *positive* side effects. Here are five areas where you'll be more focused as a result of having a daily prayer time:

1. **Reading.** Our attention can be quickly sabotaged by the constant pinging of email and social media. These short "blips" of distraction hinder our ability to sustain the attention it takes to read longer articles and books, or even past the third line of an email. By having a daily prayer time, you'll actually find that your ability to read improves.
2. **Conversations with others.** You may find that your daily prayer time impacts your ability to have meaningful

conversations with others. You'll learn to be more attentive to them, looking them in the eye with greater focus. You won't wish you were somewhere else because you'll be savoring the moment of the conversation and connection.

3. **Commuting.** Instead of checking Facebook or texting at stoplights during your commute, you'll be honing your ability to focus. You'll be more aware of your surroundings and may even be able to pray while you drive or ride. You'll also drive more safely.

4. **Doing desk work.** We all may have email to process, reports to write, or phone calls to make. Instead of trying to multi-task with partial attention, you'll catch yourself beginning to give each task your full presence. You'll find that you end up getting more done in a shorter amount of time.

5. **Doing other kinds of work.** If you're at home with young children, you'll see the level of chaos reduced simply by doing one thing at a time. If you care for others in a health-care setting, your appreciation for each patient will increase as you look each one in the eye and more deeply listen to what they're telling you.

In each of these moments during the day, you'll find that the results of your prayer time are paying dividends in ways that seem to have little to do with prayer. This is because spending more time with God in prayer leads you to be more fully present throughout your day.

IMAGINE YOUR DAY

Now let's put all of the pieces together. I'd like to show you what this can look like in your daily life.

Imagine your day going really well. You wake up at a reasonable time. You visit the bathroom and then make a cup of coffee. You might scan the news headlines on your phone while the coffee is brewing. Then, with mug in hand, you head into the living room to your favorite chair in the corner. You switch on a reading lamp and see that your Bible is right where you left it—on the table, along with your journal. The sun is coming up outside and light is starting to fill the room. The house is quiet. This begins your morning quiet time—you're ready to be alone with God.

As you've done for the past few weeks, you proceed with your quiet time, including adoration, confession, thanksgiving, and supplication. (ACTS is a helpful acronym for remembering different kinds of prayer.) Spending three to four minutes in each part, your prayer time wraps up with your eyes closed and you just sit for a few moments. It may be the only quiet moment of your day.

Not wanting to leave this space, you remember that you do have a job to get to and stand up. You eat breakfast, grab a shower, and get dressed, heading off to work forty-five minutes later. You have just laid a foundation, built on the Habit of Presence, to give God time in your day. You were fully present to God for those twenty minutes, and while you heard no audible voice from heaven nor felt anything emotional during your prayer, you showed up.

So did God.

The rest of your day isn't devoid of stress. There's the 10:00 a.m. meeting that could have easily been summed up in a memo. There's Shelly, your annoying coworker who voices what seems like every thought that comes into her head. At lunchtime you realize that in your morning rush, you forgot to make a sandwich.

Still, while you're at work, you find yourself making eye contact with others and you're listening rather than just waiting to talk. This makes sense since you spent a few minutes listening for God to speak to you through your morning quiet time. While you may not have heard an audible voice from God, you have a sense, albeit slight, that God is leading you. When someone interrupts you at your desk, you don't snap at the person. You're starting to see your work as an opportunity for ministry.

When you get home from work, you put your smartphone on the counter to charge. As for the laptop and work-related paperwork, those can wait until the kids go to bed. For now, you're being present to the ones around you. This sounds easier than it actually is, and it takes practice. Still, your daily prayer time will start to build spiritual momentum in your life.

All of this began with twenty minutes of prayer at the beginning of your day. You showed up and gave God one-third of an hour. He gave you the grace of being present to what really mattered during your day.

Here are three steps to help you apply the Habit of Presence to your life:

1. Download or print the 2nd Habit worksheet at www.mikestpierre.com/prayer.
2. Fill out the Habit of Presence worksheet, and answer the following three questions:

- When was the last time that I felt fully present to a situation or person?
- During which time of the day do I feel most alert and most engaged in what I'm doing?
- What would it look like for my prayer time to be more focused and less distracted?

3. Pray: *Lord, help me to be fully present to you when I pray. When I am with those I love and those with whom I work, let me give them my full attention. Then I will find you.*

THE 3RD HABIT
PREPARATION AND PLANNING

THE 3RD HABIT
PREPARATION AND PLANNING

My dad had his eye on it for months. He had ordered the catalog and talked it over with my mom. She couldn't understand why he needed *another* tractor. The John Deere, with its green paint and famous yellow trim, seemed to cut the lawn just fine.

"Camille, it's about more than just cutting the grass. This new tractor will help us do the snow in the winter. It's what I need to take care of the whole property, not just the lawn," said my dad, as he built the case for purchasing a bigger, better tractor. He was determined.

There was very little that the new orange Kubota didn't have. It came equipped with a front loader, a roll bar, and even a cup holder. After all, you wouldn't want to find yourself without a cold drink—or a hot one—when you're doing all that work outdoors.

Once my father had persuaded my mom that our old tractor was somehow insufficient, he had one small detail to coordinate: where to store the new one. The Kubota was taller and wider than the old John Deere. With a glimmer in his eye, my father proudly declared one night at dinner, "I've been doing a lot of thinking about the new tractor and I've finally figured out where to store it!"

The plan was to retrofit the current toolshed into a fully capable tractor garage. The entry would be widened and the space above the entry would retract upward through some sort of pulley device my dad would build. Several months later, my dad drove out of the shed with his shiny new Kubota tractor. The smile on his face said it all. His plan had worked.

My father had created a schema for his new tractor to fit into the toolshed. He had gone to sleep thinking about it. He would wake in the night with a new measurement or idea. These would be jotted down on a small sketch pad next to his bed. Because he had a goal in mind, his plans followed. This story brings us to the 3rd Habit: Preparation and Planning.

A SPIRITUAL PLAN

This concept is more difficult than it first appears to be. Planning, when it comes to the spiritual life, is rare. Sure, we might think ahead and sign up for a retreat. We might read about a well-known speaker coming to our area and reserve a seat. But beyond that, most of us have built our spiritual lives on our routines.

The good news is that routines can be improved through planning.

Let's look at weekly attendance at Mass as a practical example. With the exception of choosing which Mass to attend, I rarely put planning into this routine. As for preparation, that's where I need to improve.

You can relate to this, right? You know you shouldn't be late to Mass, but life can get in the way and you find yourself staring Catholic guilt straight in the eye. You arrive late and slink into the back of the church, hoping that no one notices.

But—here's the leap of faith that I'm asking you to take with me—*what if it were different?* What if you could imagine an entirely different Sunday Mass experience? This is precisely where preparation and planning come into play.

GETTING STARTED

Take the story of my father outfitting his shed in order to fit a larger tractor. You might think that the genius was in his plan. While important, his plan was actually the *result* of something else. His notes and designs sketched on paper were the by-products of something far more powerful: the audacity to try.

Most of us stay stuck because it's scary to try. Most of us don't pray because we aren't sure how to begin praying. We can say the same thing about giving to charity, eating more vegetables, and saving for retirement. Starting is terrifying because it always brings the possibility of failure along with it.

HOW-TO

It could be that Christians today have the right doctrines but the wrong disciplines. We know God loves us but we can't seem to figure out how to love him back. We recognize that our neighbors are created in God's image and likeness but we struggle to actually love them in practice. We get lost in the process of going from *what* we believe to *how* to behave. This is certainly the case when it comes to prayer.

The key, as it turns out, is simply to start. And then *keep* starting.

Starting is something we resist by nature. Inherent in starting anything is the possibility of failing, and failure brings embarrassment. We don't like to be embarrassed, so we don't try things. This is part biology and part psychology.

Lizard Brain

A part of our brains, sometimes called the "lizard brain," is wired to help us avoid danger. It takes over when we're in scary situations and can be quite helpful. I remember a situation when my lizard brain helped save two people on my way to work.

I was driving to the school where I served as president. After pulling off the highway, a ramp brought me around a corner and eventually to a stoplight. As I drove on the ramp, slowing down my car, I noticed a car pointed in the other direction, except that it didn't look right.

It was upside down.

The driver had apparently lost control and the car careened off the road. The car, a late-model compact, was now in a large ditch. My lizard brain kicked into high gear and I found myself parking my car, putting on the hazard lights, and sprinting to the scene of the wreck. I dialed 911 as I ran and reached the car about thirty seconds later.

I began trying to communicate with the two people inside, who seemed to be speaking Spanish. They were scrambling, trying to pull themselves up out of the car. One of the passengers, a woman in her fifties, was crying. Unsure if they were hurt, I spoke to them in the best Spanish I could muster. Not having spoken the language for years, I'm fairly certain that I told them that the police were *eating*. When the passengers looked at me with a surprised reaction, I realized my error and told them that the police were *coming*.

I then pulled the two passengers, a husband and his wife, out of the car. They were okay, and the sound of sirens let me know that they would be in good hands. I then fixed my necktie, went back to my car and off to work.

Bravery? Not really. My lizard brain had simply kicked into high gear in the face of emergency.

Resistance

My reaction at the car accident is a positive example of the lizard brain in action, but there's another side. The lizard brain can also produce what author Steven Pressfield calls resistance. Pressfield, the author of *The Legend of Bagger Vance* and sixteen other books, knows a thing or two about resistance. As a coach to other writers, he instructs them to push through resistance in order to find their voice. In *The War of Art: Break Through the Blocks & Win Your Inner Creative Battles*, he puts it this way: "The most important thing about art is to work. Nothing else matters except sitting down every day and trying."[1]

Resistance, according to Pressfield, is what the lizard brain produces when it's at its worst. It's a force inside you that tells you to stop trying and to maintain security. It wants you to play it safe and avoid all risks. While I was able to react and help the couple out of their overturned car, resistance can turn me into a wimp if I let it.

Marketing guru Seth Godin puts it this way: "Every time you find yourself following the manual instead of writing the manual, you're avoiding anguish and giving in to the resistance."[2] In other words, resistance can influence you into living more passively and without the agency that God has inherently wired into you.

DON'T SETTLE

In *Gaudete et Exsultate*, Pope Francis puts it another way: "The Lord asks everything of us, and in return he offers us true life, the happiness for which we were created. He wants us to be saints and not to settle for a bland and mediocre existence" (1). Resistance, if we let it, can nudge us toward preferring an afternoon shopping at Target to a meaningful conversation with another person. Resistance, if we let it, can tell us that a playlist on Spotify is more interesting than a moment spent reading something of genuine value. Resistance, if we let it, can convince us to place more premium on free time than on sharing our faith with someone in need. Pope Francis, once again, speaks to this struggle: "Let us ask the Lord for the grace not to hesitate when the Spirit calls us to take a step forward" (*Gaudete et Exsultate* 139).

The Habit of Preparation and Planning is all about taking one step and trusting that the Lord will eventually show us the next step.

As believers, we can now identify the areas where the 3rd Habit is especially useful. I suggest the following spaces in our spiritual lives where more preparation and planning are most needed:

1. Preparing for the morning quiet time.
2. Preparing for sacramental moments.

3. Planning the annual spiritual growth calendar.

DAILY QUIET TIME

A daily quiet time is perhaps the greatest investment you can make in your spiritual life. This isn't to say that Sunday Mass or any other celebration of the sacraments comes second. Rather, "doing the work" of becoming a saint is as much about the daily grind as it is about the public moments of grace.

Ask a top-tier athlete and they'll tell you that the competitions are important but the daily practices are even more important. These are the moments that ultimately define our progress.

THE POWER OF ROUTINE

Greg McKeown tells a story of one athlete in particular in his best-selling book *Essentialism: The Disciplined Pursuit of Less.* Michael Phelps is the most decorated Olympian of all time, with twenty-eight medals—twenty-three of them gold. We know his boyish smile and his tall, lanky swimmer's frame. What you may not be familiar with is the ritual he has used to prepare for every race.

Phelps's pre-race routine is similar to watching an old VHS tape. Put the tape into the VHS player and hit Play. No thinking. No decisions to make. For Phelps, peak performance comes from being fully engaged in the moment and having zero distractions. He learned early on as an athlete that if he could eliminate distractions, he could outperform his competition.

McKeown describes Phelps's ritual almost as if it were a religious rite. Two hours before a race, Phelps would do a particular warm-up swim. Then he would dry off, put on his headphones, and sit on the massage table—sitting, not lying down, every time. From this point on, Phelps wouldn't speak to his coach or anyone else until the race was complete. At the forty-five-minute mark before the race, he would get dressed. At the thirty-minute mark he would go to the warm-up pool for another swim. At the ten-minute mark he would walk to the prep room and find a place to sit alone, goggles on one side of him, a towel on the other. At race time he would walk to the blocks from the left—always from the left. He would then dry the block, perform the same two stretches in the same order, and then remove his right earbud. As his name was called, out came the left earbud. Only then would Phelps actually compete in the race.

You might read this and conclude that Phelps is a maniac. It sounds as if he was obsessed, as if he had one thing and one thing only in his head: winning. You would be right. His obsession resulted in twenty-eight Olympic medals.

Why did Phelps construct such an elaborate pre-race formula? Was there some magic in the music he played through his headphones? Hardly. The point of it all was to eliminate choice and take willpower out of the equation.

Remember: willpower is highly overrated. Phelps knows this as a professional athlete. You and I do too.

DESIGN YOUR ROUTINE

What if you could design a routine like Phelps did? No, I'm not talking about swimming but about your prayer life. What if you could design a morning routine that felt natural and allowed more room for prayer? With some practice, it's possible.

For starters, you can prepare for your routine the night before. For me, this is as simple as making sure the coffee maker is ready. I place one K-Cup in front of the machine as well as the exact mug I'll use. When my sorry butt gets out of bed, at least I know that a decent cup of coffee will be waiting for me.

Then I take the dog out while the coffee brews. When we get back, I head downstairs to my home office with the coffee and the dog. I then begin my morning prayers and reading, which lasts about thirty minutes.

That's it. It's nothing complicated, but this routine works so well for me that a day without it feels off-kilter. You can design something for your mornings too. The key is to think ahead of time, prepare your routine, and then carry it out. Day after day, you'll begin to build the muscle of your morning prayer routine.

PREPARE FOR THE SACRAMENTS

Another area in which you and I can improve relates to the sacraments. In my experience, the sacraments we celebrate once (for example, Baptism) are easier to prepare for than those that we receive over and over, such as the Eucharist. This isn't to say that more preparation necessarily makes for a better reception of the sacrament. I can think of dozens of teenagers I have known who prepared for their Confirmation without the grace of the sacrament taking root. Let's focus on the sacraments we celebrate often: in this case, Reconciliation and the Eucharist.

RECONCILIATION

Reconciliation has been described in this way by Pope Benedict XVI: "Those, on the other hand, who recognize that they are weak and sinful entrust themselves to God and obtain from him grace and forgiveness. It is precisely this message that must be transmitted: what counts most is to make people understand that in the Sacrament of Reconciliation, whatever the sin committed, if it is humbly recognized and the person involved turns with trust to the priest-confessor, he or she never fails to experience the soothing joy of God's forgiveness."[3]

Reconciliation is similar to an exam that you can prepare for. You know the format, or can review it. You have memorized the lines, or can use one of the widely available cheat sheets. All you need to do is humble yourself, identify your sins, and then have a good talk with your confessor. On the other hand, if we simply rush into Confession and hurry through our list of sins, it's less likely that we'll be open to the transforming grace of the sacrament. We won't change.

Be Prepared

How can we prepare for Reconciliation? The Church has some good advice in this regard. The Church is clear that making a "good confession" takes intentionality and planning. A drive-by, quickie confession isn't the goal here. A repentant, prayerful experience is what we want. Typically this involves a confession of serious and mortal sins, but it's not limited to these.

To this end, the *Catechism of the Catholic Church* recommends confessing "smaller" sins in the sacrament: "Without being strictly necessary, confession of everyday faults (venial sins) is nevertheless strongly recommended by the Church. Indeed, the regular confession of our venial sins helps us to form our conscience, fight against evil tendencies, let ourselves be healed by Christ and progress in the life of the Spirit" (*CCC*, 1458).

If you want to add even more preparation and planning to how you celebrate the sacrament, schedule it in your calendar or preferred to-do list manager. I use an autoscheduling app. All I have to do is enter "Go to Confession every month," and the app reminds me once a month. I never have to think about it after that. This is a good example of bringing a productivity tip into your spiritual life.

EUCHARIST

Now let's look at how you can bring some more preparation to your weekly experience of Mass. Be honest with me for a second: What's your typical experience of Sunday Mass? Do you arrive on time? Late? Are you usually stressed out? When was the last good homily you heard? What was it about? And how about the music?

I'll put myself out there and say that my typical Sunday Mass experience is far from ideal. I make no excuses by telling you that I have four children, that I live fifteen minutes from church, or that my wife changes her outfit three times before heading out the door. Nope—not going to be that guy. While those things are all true (even the wife part), they're not excuses for my failure to put more planning into Sunday Mass.

G. K. Chesterton once wrote, "The Mass is very long and tiresome unless one loves God."[4] If you have children, you've lived this quote. Even for those who *do* love God, Mass can be difficult. Homilies rarely land where you are in your daily life. The music seems *beige*, and the whole thing can feel rather ordinary.

Maybe it's time that we rediscover the rich blessing of the Eucharist. Mass is much more than what it feels, looks, sounds, tastes, or even smells like. Holy Communion is exactly that: holy communion with God. I'm reminded of a quote from St. John Paul II during a visit to Bologna in 1997: "The Eucharist is the secret of my day. It gives strength and meaning to all my activities of service to the Church and to the whole world. . . . Let Jesus in the Blessed Sacrament speak to your hearts. It is he who is the true answer of life that you seek."[5]

Ready for Mass

When you consider Mass in this way, it makes preparation all the more important. How can you prepare for Mass? Here are five suggestions:

1. **Read the Gospel each day.** While this is valuable to do before you attend Mass, it's also valuable to be reading the scriptures "with the Church" each day. That way, when you get to Sunday Mass, your ear is more attentive to the proclamation of the Gospel.

2. **Plan what you're going to wear the night before.** This isn't your mom talking; it's just common sense. If a smooth

morning has fewer choices built into it, it makes sense to lay out your clothes the night before.

3. **Get enough rest.** There are two good reasons for doing this. First, it will make getting up easier. Second, you're more likely to stay awake at Mass. Am I the only Catholic who has fallen asleep during Mass? I don't think so.

4. **Minimize your steps the morning of Mass.** This relates nicely to the second point about your clothes. Try to put your Sunday morning on autopilot. From your breakfast to what you wear, don't let small things get in the way of the next point.

5. **Get to church early.** There are two ways to arrive to an event: on time and in time. When you arrive *on time*, you get to Mass at 8:58 a.m. before a 9:00 a.m. Mass. When you arrive *in time*, you get there at 8:50 a.m., find a decent parking spot, and then pick out a good seat at Mass. In the latter, there's no rushing around, just good preparation. This will make your Mass experience much more pleasant and less stressful.

These are just some of the practical ways that you can put the Habit of Preparation and Planning into your Sunday worship. This takes us to the final area for planning: your annual spiritual growth calendar.

SPIRITUAL GROWTH CALENDAR

Before I began practicing strategies for spiritual growth, I knew a lot about "calendaring." I suspect you do too. You know when your best friend's birthday is. You have a sense of when to prepare your lawn for the summer. You probably have a favorite time of year. (Mine is fall.) We understand calendars intuitively.

What if you could harness that intuition and apply it to your spiritual life?

I have great news—you can, and I'll show you how. A spiritual growth calendar (SGC for short) is nothing more than a general framework for when and how you can grow in your faith; you can think of it as a scaffolding around your spiritual life. A typical SGC is made up of four doable components:

- an annual retreat
- a quarterly personal day
- a monthly spiritual direction appointment
- daily quiet time

These four things will put some serious heat under your rear end when it comes to prayer. You'll find yourself walking around with more spiritual confidence than you've ever had. Why? Because you have a plan, and that makes all the difference.

ANNUAL RETREAT

An annual retreat doesn't have to be fancy. It will probably take you away from home for one or two nights. If this isn't available to you, a day retreat is a fine option. Find a place and a format that feeds your soul. If that's a silent retreat, great. If it's a directed retreat with a group of people, that's good too.

QUARTERLY PERSONAL DAY

A quarterly personal day is most likely a foreign concept. I can hear my wife saying out loud, "Wait, you want me to take an entire day for myself four times a year?" Absolutely. Just as you would take a day for an off-site meeting at work, your relationship with the Lord deserves some quality time as well. By doing this quarterly, you'll be making a huge investment in your faith.

Instead of going to a retreat center, your quarterly personal day might be out in nature or even at home. Spend more time journaling, praying, and being with God. You might go to Confession or visit your favorite church, shrine, or monastery. Review the past few months and let God show you areas for growth and improvement. Enjoy the day. At first this will feel luxurious and you'll have some guilt. Push through that and realize that you're making more time for God. Everything else is a distant second.

MONTHLY SPIRITUAL DIRECTION

Monthly spiritual direction is the next plank in your scaffolding, your SGC. You have a spiritual director, right? If not, put this on your to-do list and mark it "urgent." A good spiritual director is like a personal trainer. He or she will kick your butt and you won't always like it, but trust me, it's worth it. Consider asking your pastor, a retired priest, a religious sister or brother, a deacon, or a lay minister to help you find someone. Note, though, that not every director is right for every directee. Give it three meetings. If the connection is weak or just doesn't fit, try someone else. Remember too that a spiritual director isn't a counselor or therapist. The purpose of spiritual direction is to discover God's will in your life and help you more fully surrender yourself to it in trust.

DAILY QUIET TIME

We've already talked a lot about this, but suffice it to say that you ought to be spending more time alone with God now than you did before you started reading this book. Much of your growth (and mine) is tied up with your daily habit of prayer. There's nothing glamorous about this, but that doesn't mean that it's unimportant.

These four components make up the SGC and form a scaffolding around your spiritual life. When you're practicing all four, God will start to open up doors like never before. You'll start noticing details that before seemed obscure. You'll relate to other people with greater reverence. Your prayer life will begin to feel more real. Best of all, the SGC can help you draw closer than ever to Jesus Christ.

Here are three steps to help you apply the Habit of Preparation and Planning to your life:

1. Download or print the 3rd Habit worksheet at www.mikestpierre.com/prayer.
2. Fill out the Habit of Preparation and Planning worksheet, and spend five minutes alone reflecting on this quote from David Allen: "In my experience, when people do more planning, more informally and naturally, they relieve a great deal of stress *and* obtain better results."[6] Do you agree with this quote? Why or why not? What is it about planning that's foreign to your spiritual life?
3. Consider the following questions. Of the areas we outlined in this chapter—the sacraments, Mass, and your spiritual growth calendar—which is most challenging to you? Why? What one thing can you do this week to become more prepared to pray and plan for your spiritual life?

THE 4TH HABIT
PERSISTENCE AND PERSEVERANCE

As a kid, who did you look up to? Truth be told, I wanted to be like Tom Selleck in *Magnum P.I.* I'm not sure if it was his fire-engine-red Ferrari or the fact that he tracked down the bad guys for a living, but man, did I admire him. It got so bad that in grade school I actually signed my name "Michael St. P.I."!

Fast-forward about thirty years and I had the opportunity to work with one of my professional heroes. Instead of a private investigator with swag and a propensity for beautiful women, my role model was a California consultant named Patrick Lencioni.

You may have heard of Patrick and his many best-selling books, which have sold more than five million copies and have been translated into thirty languages. The first book of his I picked up was *The Five Dysfunctions of a Team*, and I've been reading Patrick's books ever since. His writing style is down-to-earth, and he has a quick sense of humor. When I later learned that he is a devout Catholic, I was all the more inspired.

When our organization invited Patrick to join our board, I think I told the person inviting him that if she got Patrick to say yes, I would drive across the country to thank her. I made the wise choice of flying instead. Since then I've had the pleasure of working with Patrick in various capacities. One in particular stands out.

BLINDSIDED

I was scheduled to fly to Patrick's office in Oakland, California, along with two other board members. The plan was to hammer out a strategic vision for our organization—in seven hours. It seemed impossible to me, but Patrick was confident that it could be done. Out I went, full of optimism.

Much of that optimism flew out the window as the day unfolded. We met, planned, discussed, and debated. We wrote on the whiteboard. We crossed things out. We prayed. We ate. We crossed more things out and ate even more food.

I should mention that Patrick has tremendous physical stamina. Almost oblivious to his surroundings, he can work for seven hours without taking a break.

It was just before dinner when things got bad.

Patrick became increasingly frustrated with our meeting. He felt we were being too wishy-washy and lacked the courage to make tough decisions. Things got loud: he shouted, and I shouted back. Our other two board members sat in shock. I could see Magnum's Ferrari leaving the TV screen and taking my career along with it.

In the most heated moment—one I'll never forget—Patrick pointed his finger at me and yelled, "You're a weak leader!"

RESPONSE

To make it worse, Patrick ended the meeting and invited all of us to dinner to "celebrate the day's progress." All I wanted was to hide under a table and lick my wounds. How could I sit across the table from someone who had just told me I was weak? Obviously I'd have to find another hero.

Patrick's words seared my heart and made a home in my mind. If he had told me that Boston is the worst sports town, that would have been painful. Or if he had said that my children were ugly, or that my minivan made my butt look fat, those things would have upset me too. *But my professional street cred?* No one had ever questioned *that* before. *Not ever.*

The whole thing shook me to the core and I went to bed with two thoughts:

1. I'm loved by God and that's where my deepest identity lies.
2. I won't let anyone else define my dignity.

The next day I sent Patrick an email defending myself. He responded with an apology and a request to talk on the phone during the week. We had that conversation, and in the months that followed we made up and moved on.

MEETING THE CHALLENGE

That meeting with Patrick was one of the most difficult in my professional career. I wouldn't want to relive it for any amount of money. Still, it forced me to come to a sobering conclusion: Patrick was right.

I *had* been a weak leader and one who was too worried about keeping everyone happy. I had a choice to make: either buck up and get tough, or give in and remain a soft, less-than-inspiring leader.

Thankfully, and by God's grace, I chose the former. The insight I had that night in my hotel room—that I'm loved by God and that I won't let anyone else define my dignity—has stayed with me. Today Patrick and I are friends. His courage to deliver some hard truth was what I needed at the time, and I credit him for a turning point in my career. That brings us to the 4th Habit: Persistence and Perseverance.

PERSISTENCE AND MIND-SET

Persistence isn't the most attractive quality a person can have. As a leader, I'd much rather be described as visionary, bold, or creative. Still, research tells us that persistence is one of the most important qualities in life, including prayer life.

First, let's examine what we know about the objective truth of persistence. Persistence is closely tied to mind-set. This isn't to say that your "success" is a result of your attitude. Mind-set is slightly different from attitude. Attitude is your disposition from an emotional perspective; mind-set is a belief in your capacity to grow and learn.

Best-selling author Carol Dweck illustrates this point in her book *Mindset: The New Psychology of Success*: "When you enter a mindset, you enter a new world. In one world—the world of fixed traits—success is about proving you're smart or talented.

Validating yourself. In the other—the world of changing qualities—it's about stretching yourself to learn something new. Developing yourself."[1] Persistence, then, is a useful tool for accomplishing meaningful activities. Much trial and error is required for nearly all difficult tasks. If you want to pray, you'll need persistence in spades.

STRETCHING TOWARD SUCCESS

Before I began working in higher education, my career was focused on middle and secondary schools. Twice a year our leadership team had what we called the "student review meeting." This fancy name captured the essence of sitting in a room for three hours to evaluate our students' successes and struggles. We looked at how hundreds of students were doing and tried to understand what was helping them succeed or causing them to fail.

The conversations often went like this:

Principal: Why do we feel that Brenda is struggling in calculus but seems to have no trouble in advanced placement history?

Dean of Students: Well, she's having troubles at home.

Dean of Guidance: I know that she has a good rapport with her history teacher.

Dean of Athletics: If you take away her place on the softball team, that's all she has to feel good about herself. It's her passion!

The ninja strategy used by schools to determine what makes Brenda succeed in one class but exhibit poor effort in another is the secret sauce of learning. Is it the teacher? Is Brenda simply not capable of learning math? Has her learning "topped out," or can we unlock some next gear in her capacity as a student? Is it her schedule? These questions and more flood the minds of school administrators and teachers.

For the student review meetings, this is where persistence came into play. We simply didn't give up.

LEARN TO BUILD PATIENCE

Many Americans are led to believe that students of Asian descent are better in math than their Caucasian counterparts. I've certainly heard the parking lot chatter from parents: "That boy is better in math because he's Chinese." An uncomfortable quiet comes over the crowd until someone changes the subject.

But are Asian students better in math?

Malcolm Gladwell wanted to answer this very question in his book *Outliers: The Story of Success*. Like many of us, Gladwell wondered if Asian students are indeed genetically better in mathematics. After all, students from Hong Kong, Japan, South Korea, Taiwan, and Singapore tend to do dramatically better on math exams such as the TIMSS assessment than do their counterparts from other developed countries. Why is that?

Gladwell's answer stems from the study of rice farming, an industry close to the heart of much of Asian civilization. Building a rice paddy, in case you didn't know, is quite difficult. Contrast this with our contemporary understanding of planting crops: When I think of farming, I see a field plowed in straight lines. Next, the seeds are inserted into the troughs, then covered over, watered, and fertilized. Finally, things grow.

A rice paddy is different. It's more time-consuming and demanding and less forgiving. While it's not difficult to grow a small rice plant on your windowsill, an entire paddy (or field of paddies) takes precision and patience. Rice farmers have no vacations, and only to the degree that they tend to their paddies do they benefit. Some estimate that the average workload of a rice farmer is three thousand hours per year. Gladwell proposes that the first influence on an Asian student's ability to do math is the student's cultural appreciation for patience and persistence, stemming from rice agriculture.

The second influence is the Chinese number system, which is highly regular and has no exceptions in its linguistic structure—counting, addition, and subtraction are more logical tasks than they are in the irregular language of the Western number system. Gladwell suggests that because the basic tasks are easier in the Chinese number system, Asian children are more likely to do calculations faster and correctly, then more likely to enjoy math because they're good at it, then more likely to try harder because they enjoy it. Their initial ease and a certain level of enjoyment sustain their patience with more difficult math problems.

This patient approach to learning, over time, produces what is popularly known as *grit*.

GRIT

The expert in grit is Angela Duckworth. Her book *Grit: The Power of Passion and Perseverance* provides a convincing view of a person's ability to learn something when it would be considered difficult. Her TED talk on the same subject has been viewed some ten million times. She defines grit as "the tendency to sustain interest in and effort toward very long-term goals."[2] The intersection between interest and effort is where the magic happens.

Duckworth shares some interesting data from her study of West Point army cadets. With all the intellectual and physical effort that it takes to receive an appointment to West Point, one would think that a cadet would do *absolutely everything* in his or her power to ensure success. Surprisingly, this isn't the case. In fact, during the "Beast Barracks" seven-week training, some students drop out, despite being bright, capable, fit, and driven to success.[3] They persist enough to *get there*, but they fail in the perseverance it takes to *stay there*.

PERSEVERANCE

Duckworth wanted to know why some high achievers ended up dropping out. She's not the only one. I can't understand why professional athletes throw away promising careers in the pursuit of lesser things. We see it all the time—a college sensation becomes a mediocre professional. Why is that?

Duckworth's conclusion is that those who survived Beast Barracks didn't have more brains or brawn than those who dropped out—they simply had more grit. They were able to be persistent *over the long haul*. That's perseverance.

Grit isn't isolated to Asian students doing math problems or students at a military service academy. Certain countries seem to produce grittier students than others. Finland, for example, is regarded as having the best schools in the world. Year after year they outperform countries such as the United States in the PISA test. An article in *Time* magazine described Finnish grit this way: "It is a compound of bravado and bravery, of ferocity and tenacity, of the ability to keep fighting after most people would have quit, and to fight with the will to win."[4] The article was written in 1940.

YOUR OWN PATH

How does grit apply to our spiritual lives? It's here that we turn to the saints and my friend Mary.

Mary, who I met in college, is one of the most spiritual individuals I've ever known. She had a strong devotion to St. Thérèse of Lisieux. She had read Thérèse's autobiography, *The Story of a Soul*, and was an evangelist for the saint's "little way" of doing small things with great love. She would routinely quote Thérèse and ask for her intercession for her studies, relationships, and family. Let me put it this way: Mary wanted to be like Thérèse in every way she could muster.

Then something happened. Several years later, I saw Mary and asked her about her devotion to the "Little Flower." What she said surprised me and stuck with me in the twenty years since. She said, "I think Thérèse sort of messed me up."

As we talked further, she shared that she had modeled her entire life around Thérèse. As she grew older, she concluded that God wanted her to find her own path, not simply replicate the spirituality of Thérèse. This was a hard realization for Mary but one with which she ultimately came to terms. That required not only honesty but also grit.

LEARN FROM THE SAINTS

The saints are tremendous models of faith that we can imitate but not really copy. I took my dog to a local park and struck up a conversation with a man from India. While he wasn't a Christian, he shared how St. Teresa of Kolkata was widely admired in India. Real saints are like that—even those who don't share their faith admire them. You don't have to be Catholic to appreciate the sacrifice of St. Maximilian Kolbe in Auschwitz or St. John Paul II's brave journey through Parkinson's disease.

We try our best not just to honor the saints but also to learn from them. The Church is clear as to the immense value the saints bring to our lives as role models and guides. Echoing this invitation to an admirable life, Pope Benedict XVI said in 2007: "Holiness does not consist in never having erred or sinned. Holiness increases the capacity for conversion, for repentance, for willingness to start again and, especially, for reconciliation and forgiveness."[5] This depth of conversion reminds us of the immense value of grit, persistence, and perseverance in the spiritual life.

We also need to find our own unique relationship with God. In so doing, we can find holiness attainable. Like Mary, we need to find our own *style* of living as adult believers. It takes some spiritual grit to persevere over the long haul and be patient with our own sanctification. Pope Francis, in *Gaudete et Exsultate*, speaks to this: "We should not grow discouraged before examples of holiness that appear unattainable. There are some testimonies that may prove helpful and inspiring, but that we are not meant to copy, for that could even lead us astray from the one specific path that the Lord has in mind for us" (11).

Look up to the saints, but don't think for a minute that your road is going to be exactly like theirs—or worse, that it *should be*. It's going to be better because it's uniquely yours. What makes your spiritual path wonderful, however, is also what makes it difficult. When I asked a priest friend what was the most difficult thing about his prayer life, he said, "Sticking with it."

I suggest that there are two specific areas of our spiritual lives that are most in need of the Habit of Persistence and Perseverance: parish membership and daily prayer.

Parish Membership

Parish membership doesn't mean the same thing to me now that it did when I was a kid. We went to St. Mary's in Georgetown, Massachusetts, which was a cavernous church about ten minutes from our home. If we arrived early, we would sit in the car and wait until about forty-five seconds before the Mass would start. God forbid that we might want to get inside earlier!

Our parish was where we "got" the sacraments. The community aspect? Not so much. I don't blame my parents; at least we went to Mass. I don't really blame the pastor either, although he wasn't particularly effective at leading his local flock. Our consumer mind-set limited how we practiced our faith. Back then, the parish was where you went if you needed to receive a sacrament. Thankfully we understand parish membership more deeply today. We know that it's an expression of adult participation in a faith community. We know that it helps us grow more fully as disciples. We see ourselves as contributors, not just consumers.

One program, ESTEEM, is designed by the National Leadership Roundtable on Church Management to help college students prepare for parish service and leadership once they graduate. The program provides realistic advice and guidance about finding a good parish and becoming fully engaged as a member. Another ministry, the Duke Catholic Center, teaches that registering as a member is one of the marks of a mature adult believer. In short, we know today that parish membership ought to mean something and should nudge us into responsible participation in the faith community.

The problem is that, in many parishes, there's only a partial framework in place to engage the faithful. Preaching isn't as interesting as we'd like it to be. The music may not be to our taste. The spirit of hospitality varies from Mass to Mass. As for a systematic process of welcoming new parishioners? Very few churches have this in place. Put all of this together and it can be hard to persevere as a member of a parish.

The University of Notre Dame Institute on Church Life hosted an event in the fall of 2017 called "Cultures of Formation." The main question the five hundred or so participants sought to answer was stunning: Why would a young person want to remain Catholic as they get older? With talks ranging from speakers such as Bishop Robert Barron to author Nicholas Carr, the audience wrestled with the issue of faith perseverance in the face of what is mostly mediocre parish life.

But what if it were different? What if you could participate in a parish community that was consistently welcoming? What if you could help your parish priests get feedback that actually helped them preach better homilies? What if you could be a parishioner others wanted to learn from and emulate?

Author Chris Lowney puts it this way: "Our church is facing its greatest crisis in five centuries. . . . We are all co-responsible for the church's being and action, and it has never been more necessary of all of us to step in and lead."[6] You and I have a valuable role to play in being perseverant, generative members of our parishes.

Obstacles to Daily Prayer

This perseverance in parish life can spill over into our daily prayer life. Why is it so difficult to pray daily? I suggest five reasons:

1. **The tyranny of the urgent.** If you tell me that my daughter Ella has fallen and is bleeding, I'm going to drop everything and run to help her. That's urgent! Things that aren't urgent, we struggle with. We feel as if we can put things off for another day. We don't feel very badly about procrastinating long-term things. We put them out of our mind. I know that I'm guilty of this.

   Yet as understandable as it is to put off prayer due to a lack of urgency, a serious disciple recognizes that prayer builds relationship. Like our human relationships, prayer makes intimacy possible. If I'm talking and listening to Cary, my wife, on a daily basis, good things will follow. This isn't very hard since we have a great marriage. But if for some reason I stop listening to her and stop telling her about my day, our marriage will be in trouble. While infidelity and financial issues sidetrack many marriages, it's a lack of communication that kills the rest. Don't let your relationship with God veer off the tracks due to a lack of prayer.

2. **We lack confidence.** Ask me to talk about prayer and I'm good—I have confidence and knowledge to do so, at least to a point. But ask me to talk about car repair and I begin to sweat. I don't have confidence and feel inept when it comes to engines, carburetors, and fuel injection. The good news? Unlike car repair (at which I'll likely never succeed), a prayer life is something that I can improve daily with minimal effort. The more you show up for prayer, the more confident you'll be.

3. **We lack coaching.** Think of the last time you had a good coach, a person who got the best out of you, pushing and encouraging you to do your best. I suspect that your

performance was the best it ever was as a result. In our prayer lives, arguably the most important area of our lives, we lack adequate coaching in order to answer this question, "Am I doing it right?"

A prayer or faith coach, also called a spiritual director, can give you feedback and pointers for improvement. You're more likely to floss when you know you'll be seeing the dentist; similarily, a spiritual director will hold you accountable and help take your prayer life to the next level.

4. **We have very few peers who talk about prayer.** I'm not talking about the saints. What we have here is a lack of people *we actually know* who are praying daily and talking about it. If my buddy drives an SUV and tells me about it, I'm going to start noticing SUVs. The power of influence is immense. If I talk to my buddy about prayer, I have no doubt that he's going to remember that.

   How do you talk about prayer? One easy way is to tell someone that you're praying for them. I'll often get someone's name in my mind during my morning quiet time and then shoot them a text, just telling them that I'm praying for them. Another way to talk about prayer is to ask someone, especially when they're going through a hard time, if they've prayed about it. Again, the power of suggestion holds true.

   Finally, we can talk more about prayer by sharing with others what we're reading. If I'm reading a book by Bishop Barron, I want to tell someone about it, which will likely lead to a conversation about spiritual topics, including prayer.

5. **Human frailty.** It can be hard to persevere in prayer simply as a result of our human weakness. Because we're sinful, we're imperfect and our prayer lives reflect that. Don't let this get in the way of an honest, persistent, and perseverant pursuit of God.

Here are three steps to help you apply the Habit of Persistence and Perseverance to your life:

1. Download or print the 4th Habit worksheet at www.mikest-pierre.com/prayer.

2. Fill out the Habit of Persistence and Perseverance worksheet, and spend five minutes alone reflecting on this quote from Pope Francis: "Do not be afraid of holiness. It will take away none of your energy, vitality or joy. On the contrary, you will become what the Father had in mind when he created you, and you will be faithful to your deepest self" (*Gaudete et Exsultate* 32).

3. Look for an opportunity to find help developing your prayer life, such as joining a parish prayer group, meeting with a spiritual director, or committing to prayer time with a friend or family member.

THE 5TH HABIT
PONDERING

Off-site retreats are common in the business world. They usually last for one or two workdays and are held in a nice location far from the workplace. They're meant to help coworkers connect more deeply and give space for a different kind of thinking by pushing the pause button on everyday schedules.

Sometimes "off-sites," as they're commonly known, get a bad rap. Every few years, you'll hear of a company that spends way too much money on its off-site under the guise of team building, or my favorite activity, "strategic thinking time." Off-site critiques usually center on expense. Buffer, the social media scheduling company, famously spent more than $100,000 on an off-site, but that was due in part to the fact that their workforce is remote.[1] A closer look reveals that Buffer schedules a corporate off-site every year and feels that the benefit is well worth the cost.

An off-site can be a great idea for teams both large and small. The key is to prepare the team well in advance, facilitate the meetings well, and then follow through. *Harvard Business Review* has an excellent road map for making your next off-site effective, one that provides guidance from sixty days prior to an event.[2] I've taken teams to retreat houses, restaurants, and country clubs. Each time, we ate well, prayed, and talked a lot about important things we usually didn't have time to discuss. Year after year our teams grew smarter, more tactically astute, and more united as a whole.

But here's the question: If an off-site can work for your workplace team, what can it do for you as an individual? What if you could design an off-site just for yourself?

PERSONAL OFF-SITES

This is where we introduce the 5th Habit—Pondering.

When you ponder something, you step back and take stock of things. You assess and evaluate. You pause long enough to take a breath or two. It's a valuable practice in business but even more so in your own life of faith. The problem is that many of us don't think that our spiritual lives need structure, so building in time to ponder is rare.

I recommend that personal off-sites occur annually, quarterly, and then weekly. If this sounds impossible, think again. As I was conducting some of the research for this book, I discovered that many of the holiest people I've known take off-site retreats very seriously.

My friend Fr. Dennis takes one day a month at a local hermitage. This is his opportunity to be alone with the Lord, catch up on some reading, and think deeply about—that is, ponder—the issues he's facing. Each time he comes back with new vigor. His homilies are fresh and his call to ministry is renewed. That's what a personal off-site can do.

HOW TO OFF-SITE

Talking about a personal off-site is easy. Doing it on a regular basis, however, takes some practice. I suggest the following:

- **Annually.** This kind of off-site is often called a retreat. Look for a retreat center close to where you live or even in your parish. For example, my parish offers an annual "Day of Recollection for Men." Annual retreats often span a few days and are led by a facilitator, sometimes called a retreat "master." If you're a person who can go to an event without knowing anyone, you may have more options at your disposal. If you prefer to have a wingman at your side, local venues might be best. Still, a location that takes you out of your daily schedule is quite valuable.
- **Quarterly.** Want to go deeper? Think of a quarterly off-site as a "deep dive," lasting four or five hours once every three months. You might find a quiet spot at the beach, go for a hike in the mountains, or simply be at home where it's quiet. The key is to schedule this day in your calendar and decide in advance what you'd like to ponder. You may have a stack of

books or articles you've been putting off reading—take these with you. You may want to tackle some long-form writing. As the annual retreat is about infusing your prayer life with new oxygen, the quarterly off-site is a checkup to make sure that all your spiritual organs are functioning.

- **Weekly.** You've probably heard of honoring the Lord by keeping the Sabbath. Here we combine that with a full day without gadgets. No cell phone. No Wi-Fi. No TV. Of all the things that I do in a given month, the most powerful action I take is to use every Sunday for a digital sabbath. I find that my ability to listen improves and the conversations I have with my family are richer and more intentional. Because I'm not distracted by my smartphone, I'm fully present to the Lord and to those around me. This practice reinforces your prayer life and draws you to spend even more time on Sunday in prayer.

- **Daily.** Not surprisingly, here we revisit the idea of a daily quiet time. By steady faithfulness to your daily prayer time (typically in the morning or evening), you're incorporating the Habit of Pondering into your day. This, in turn, impacts your work and informs your schedule.

JESUS PONDERED

Whether you experiment with an annual retreat or a digital sabbath, it's important to remember that these habits are modeled on the example of Jesus. He routinely went away to deserted places for a while and then returned, ready for the next stage of his ministry. Our personal retreats should be similar.

Mark's gospel portrays the very start of Jesus' public ministry as one rooted in prayer: "Rising very early before dawn, he left and went off to a deserted place, where he prayed. Simon and those who were with him pursued him and on finding him said, 'Everyone is looking for you.' He told them, 'Let us go on to the nearby villages that I may preach there also. For this purpose have I come.' So he went into their synagogues, preaching and driving out demons throughout the whole of Galilee" (Mark 1:35–39).

Notice here the resolve with which Jesus acts. While others are worrying about crowds, Jesus calmly transitions from prayer to work. Wouldn't it be wonderful if our days had the same dynamic!

THE APOSTLES PONDERED

Consider Mark 6:30–33, which provides a glimpse of Jesus gradually teaching his followers to withdraw in prayer. "The apostles gathered together with Jesus and reported all they had done and taught. He said to them, 'Come away by yourselves to a deserted place and rest a while.' People were coming and going in great numbers, and they had no opportunity even to eat. So they went off in the boat by themselves to a deserted place. People saw them leaving and many came to know about it. They hastened there on foot from all the towns and arrived at the place before them."

JUST STOP

Amid a hectic schedule, have you ever felt that your day didn't even have thirty minutes to allow you to enjoy lunch? Do you have so many meetings that you feel as if you can hardly breathe? Jesus could relate, and as a result he pulled back for periods of time to "rest a while." We need to do the same.

I'm reminded of the 1998 movie *A Civil Action*, in which a crusty attorney played by Robert Duvall practices a daily time of sabbath. The break in Duvall's day occurs during lunch in the basement of the Harvard Law Library. When a staffer interrupts him during lunch, he responds: "If I were you, I'd make it a point in that lunch hour I'd find a place that's quiet and peaceful and I'd be away from all the noisiness and insanity, have a sandwich, read a magazine, maybe listen on a radio to a game at Fenway if it was playing at the time, and I'd make sure everyone knew that I didn't want to be disturbed in that hour of solitude because that would be my time, my own private time."[3]

ESSENTIAL PONDERING

When we talk about the Habit of Pondering, we're not talking about something that's nice to do. Rather, we're practicing a habit that is essential to a prayerful person. By stepping away from the hustle and bustle of life, we place our relationship with the Lord at the center of our lives. He then sends us back into our day with renewed vigor and confidence.

RHYTHM OF REST

Luke's gospel portrays a back-and-forth rhythm to Jesus' ministry: "The report about him spread all the more, and great crowds assembled to listen to him and to be cured of their ailments, but he would withdraw to deserted places to pray" (5:15–16). Jesus understood that his union with the Father was essential. As a result, he would regularly spend time alone in prayer.

Sometimes Jesus' prayer would continue for long stretches at a time. In Luke 6:12, we see a biblical all-nighter: "In those days he departed to the mountain to pray, and he spent the night in prayer to God."

The saints grasped this prioritizing as well: Their lives were full of prayer and work. Reflecting on the need to withdraw from an often frenetic world, Thomas Merton wrote, "We live in a society whose whole policy is to excite every nerve in the human body and keep it at the highest pitch of artificial tension, to strain every human desire to the limit and to create as many new desires and synthetic passions as possible."[4] Merton, seeing the noise of the world, worked to make contemplative prayer attainable for the everyday person.

Pope John Paul II, known for his engaging personality and love of crowds, provides another example of balancing time for prayer with the demands of work. When he was first named a bishop, Karol Wojtyła slipped into an Ursuline convent in Warsaw to spend several hours before the Blessed Sacrament because "he had many things to discuss with the Lord." Soon after he was elected pope, several members of his household became worried when he had seemingly disappeared. Instead, he was prostrate before the Lord in a private chapel, away from the noise of ordinary Vatican foot traffic.[5]

A NEW SOLITUDE

The Habit of Pondering does more than just insert periods of prayer into our days. It also renews our spirit and fills us with joy. Pope Francis talks much about this in *Gaudete et Exsultate*. He describes a new kind of solitude, fitting for our day: "We need a spirit of holiness capable of filling both our solitude and our service, our personal life and our evangelizing efforts, so that every moment can be an expression of self-sacrificing love in the Lord's eyes" (31).

Here are four steps to help you apply the Habit of Pondering to your life:

1. Download or print the 5th Habit worksheet at www.mikest-pierre.com/prayer.

2. Fill out the Habit of Pondering worksheet, and spend five minutes alone reflecting on this quote from Dorothy Day: "The thing to remember is not to read so much or talk so much about God but to talk to God."[6]
3. Look at the next three months on your calendar. When can you schedule a day to get away and be alone with God?
4. The next time someone invites you to a retreat, seriously consider attending. The next time you come across an ad for a retreat, seek more information about it.

CONCLUSION

PROGRESS OVER PERFECTION

If you've made it this far, you recognize the importance (and possibility) of progress when it comes to prayer. Progress, as it turns out, is the plus-one when it comes to the 5 Habits, and there's no better example of it than Terry Hershey.

Hershey is a best-selling author and popular speaker on topics ranging from prayer to work-life balance. Having interviewed Terry, I've found him to be humble, as he often asked me questions in the midst of a conversation. He, the supposed expert on work-life balance, is quick to point out his own flaws.

Terry is what you call a recovering workaholic. His book *The Power of Pause: Becoming More by Doing Less* outlines his maturation as a Christian. Once a pastor, Terry nearly lost it all as burnout and overwork consumed him. Now, many years later, he has become a teacher for those who are ambitious and yet want to lead a balanced, faith-filled life. His solution to preventing burnout? Transform the everyday and ordinary tasks into prayer. His advice is simple enough: "This week, embrace the mundane acts, such as washing dishes, pulling weeds, commuting, walking the dog. Consider them a form of prayer."[1]

BE PERFECT?

Progress over Perfection is the attitude we need to sustain us as we build the five habits we've discussed. We Christians struggle with both the concept and the practical application of progress. It's not that we don't try to improve but that we have difficulty being patient with our own progress. We hear Jesus say, "So be perfect, just as your heavenly Father is perfect" (Mt 5:48), and we may lose hope, or we think we're supposed to perfect ourselves. We also assume that others, who seem to be better Christians than we are, have done exactly that.

Pope Francis's 2018 apostolic exhortation *Gaudete et Exsultate* has a lot to say about this problem. The Holy Father is clear on the value of the saints in the Catholic tradition. They inspire us, providing an "exemplary imitation of Christ" (1). On the other hand, they can leave us feeling inadequate. Have you ever heard someone talk about St. Teresa of Kolkata and thought to yourself, *I'll never be as good as she was?* I certainly have.

NO EXCUSES

Rather than thinking of the saints as people without flaws, we should remember that "not everything he or she does is authentic or perfect" (*Gaudete et Exsultate* 23). Our path, the path to holiness, is committed to progress, not perfection. Progress is something *we* can achieve by doing our part to cooperate with God's grace. Perfection is what God has promised that *he* will achieve in us.

God gives each one of us everything we need to be holy. The pope speaks to this issue and reminds us that "we are frequently tempted to think that holiness is only for those who can withdraw from ordinary affairs to spend much time in prayer" (14). This, Pope Francis explains, is ultimately an excuse. That is because each one of us is "called to be holy by living our lives with love and by bearing witness in everything we do, wherever we find ourselves" (14). In other words, wherever you are, be all there. Turn your everyday into an opportunity for prayer.

STEADY GROWTH

Instead of expecting to become holy in one fell swoop, the pope suggests a more gradual path: "This holiness to which the Lord calls you will grow through small gestures" (16). In this way, "led by God's grace, we shape by many small gestures the holiness God has willed for us" (18). This is good news for progress seekers! All we have to do is stay the course.

Progress, however, requires dedication and patience: "You cannot grow in holiness without committing yourself, body and soul, to giving your best to this endeavour" (25). Our prayer life is worth the effort. Indeed, it may be the most important work of our lives.

TYING IT ALL TOGETHER

The attitude of Progress over Perfection is the perfect ribbon tied around the five habits, and it forms what I call the progress mind-set: a perspective that equips us to be comfortable with growth in steps. Look at how a progress mind-set undergirds each of the habits we've discussed:

- The 1st Habit: Passion and Pursuit. A progress mind-set is valuable so that we see our passion for the Lord unfolding gradually over time and are able to pursue that passion in practical and sustainable ways.
- The 2nd Habit: Presence. A progress mind-set recognizes the value of simply showing up each day, one prayer at a time.
- The 3rd Habit: Preparation and Planning. A progress mind-set appreciates and makes use of the little things that contribute to prayer.

- The 4th Habit: Persistence and Perseverance. A progress mind-set enables us to overcome obstacles to prayer in our lives and get back to prayer, even when we've neglected to give the Lord the time he deserves.
- The 5th Habit: Pondering. A progress mind-set provides gratitude as we look back over the past week or month and see all that God has done in our lives.

PROGRESS MOTIVATES

Progress in the spiritual life humbles us and floods our hearts with gratitude. I can't think of a better way to grow in prayer than to learn to appreciate any and all progress we make in our spiritual lives. This is nothing more than seeing what God is doing in us and through us every day. When we do so, we can be content with who and where we are and trust God to bring us to perfection in his way and in his time.

My prayer for you is that you'll return to your busy, everyday life with an even greater desire to pray, knowing that you now have the tools that you need to pray and pray well. This doesn't mean that it will be easy to maintain an active prayer life. Nonetheless, Jesus' response to an expert in the law is telling: "'Teacher, which commandment in the law is the greatest?' He said to him, 'You shall love the Lord, your God, with all your heart, with all your soul, and with all your mind. This is the greatest and the first commandment. The second is like it: You shall love your neighbor as yourself. The whole law and the prophets depend on these two commandments'" (Mt 22:36–40).

So long as your prayer is directed toward God, it's directed toward love. When you cultivate the 5 Habits of Prayerful People you'll have done your part. Then look out, because it's God's turn to do his!

ACKNOWLEDGMENTS

This book would not have been possible without the many readers of my blog over the past decade. Thank you for giving me the privilege of helping you in some small way, even when my thoughts were not fully formed.

I am grateful for the priests who have blessed my life in so many ways through their example and friendship: Fr. Dennis Berry, S.T.; Fr. Michael Martin, O.F.M. Conv.; Fr. Terry Moran, C.S.S.R.; Fr. Kevin Kennedy; and Fr. Joseph Petrillo.

Thank you to those who believed that another book on prayer was not only possible but necessary, including Lisa Hendey, Jared Dees, and my exceptionally charitable editor Jaymie Stuart Wolfe. The entire team at Ave Maria Press has been stellar.

Those who have been featured in this book have touched my life in both small and large ways: Chris Lowney, Michael Sliwinski, Christine and Kevin O'Brien, David Allen, Curtis Martin, Laura Stack, Christopher West, Shawn Blanc, Terry Hershey, and Patrick Lencioni.

The prayerful examples of Jason Simon (Evangelical Catholic), Gordy DeMarais (Saint Paul's Outreach), and Curtis Martin (FOCUS) remind me that there is still much work to be done in prayer and on campuses across the country. Thank you to Gene Monterastelli, Tom Burnford, Peter Koritansky, and Allan Wright for being friends over the long haul.

I first learned to pray through the example of my mom and dad. They provided a foundation strong enough for a lifetime. My brothers, Mark and Paul, are not only role models but friends. Thanks for allowing me to pray for your families.

Thank you to my wife, Cary, and our amazing four children, Grace, Thomas, Ella, and Benjamin. Every time you stumbled across your dad in prayer, you reminded me of what's truly important in life.

NOTES

Introduction

1. Richard Kaufman, "Prayer," *Christianity Today*, June 10, 2002, https://www.christianitytoday.com/ct/2002/june10/22.47.html.

How to Use This Book

1. *The Life of St. Teresa of Jesus*, 8:5.
2. *The Way of Perfection*, St. Teresa of Jesus, Chapter 21.
3. John Paul II, "Meeting with the Young People of New Orleans," Libreria Editrice Vaticana, September 12, 1987, para. 8, 10, https://w2.vatican.va/content/john-paul-ii/en/speeches/1987/september/documents/hf_jp-ii_spe_19870912_giovani-new-orleans.html.
4. John Paul II, "Meeting with the Young People of New Orleans," Libreria Editrice Vaticana, September 12, 1987, para. 12, https://w2.vatican.va/content/john-paul-ii/en/speeches/1987/september/documents/hf_jp-ii_spe_19870912_giovani-new-orleans.html.

Prayer and Productivity

1. Dictionary.com, s.v. "life hack," https://www.dictionary.com/browse/lifehack?s=t.
2. Natalie Goodman, "James Dyson Is Using Failure to Drive Success," Entrepreneur, November 5, 2012, https://www.entrepreneur.com/article/224855.

The 1st Habit: Passion and Pursuit

1. Steve Jobs, "2005 Stanford University Commencement Address" (speech, Stanford University, Stanford, CA, June 12, 2005), https://news.stanford.edu/2005/06/14/jobs-061505.
2. Richard N. Bolles, *What Color Is Your Parachute? A Practical Manual for Job-Hunters and Career-Changers* (New York: Ten Speed Press, 2014).
3. Cal Newport, "The Passion Trap: How the Search for Your Life's Work Is Making Your Working Life Miserable," Calnewport.com, October 16, 2010, http://calnewport.com/blog/2010/10/16/the-passion-trap-how-the-search-for-your-lifes-work-is-making-your-working-life-miserable.
4. Daniel H. Pink, *Drive: The Surprising Truth about What Motivates Us* (New York: Riverhead Books, 2009), 146.
5. Augustine, *Sermo* 56,6,9:PL 38,381.
6. Augustine, *Confessions* 1.1.
7. Catherine of Siena, *The Dialogue of Catherine of Siena*, chapt. 54.
8. Catherine of Siena, *The Dialogue of Catherine of Siena*.
9. Francis de Sales, *An Introduction to the Devout Life*, xiii.
10. "Here's to the Hearts That Ache . . . (Some Thoughts on 'La La Land')." http://corproject.com/193-heres-to-the-hearts-that-ache-some-thoughts-on-la-la-land.
11. Thérèse of Lisieux, *Manuscrits autobiographiques*, C 25r.

The 2nd Habit: Presence

1. John of the Cross, *Dark Night of the Soul*, trans. E. Allison Peers (Ingersoll, ON: Devoted Publishing, 2016), 57.

2. Renz Ofiaza, "Beyonce and Selena Gomez Rule Instagram's 2017 Year in Review," Highsnobiety, November 29, 2017, https://www.highsnobiety.com/p/instagram-2017-year-in-review.

3. Lucy Yang, "This Couple Exposed the Reality behind 'Perfect' Instagram Photos," Independent, November 7, 2017, https://www.independent.co.uk/travel/news-and-advice/instagram-perfect-travel-photos-myth-exposed-lauren-bullen-jack-morris-a8041956.html.

4. Amy Anderson, "Chip and Joanna Gaines Are Ready to Risk It All," *Success*, December 5, 2017, https://www.success.com/chip-and-joanna-gaines-are-ready-to-risk-it-all.

5. Melissa Michaels, *Love the Home You Have: Simple Ways to . . . Embrace Your Style, Get Organized, Delight in Where You Are* (Eugene, OR: Harvest House Publishers, 2015).

6. Amy Robaton, "Why So Many Americans Hate Their Jobs," MoneyWatch, March 31, 2017, https://www.cbsnews.com/news/why-so-many-americans-hate-their-jobs.

7. Jane Burnett, "Majority of Employees Are Unhappy at Work, Study Finds," Ladders, October 16, 2017, https://www.theladders.com/career-advice/majority-unhappy-at-work.

8. Scott Tousley, "Research Proves a Gratitude Journal (Strangely) Boosts Productivity," *Hubspot* (blog), last modified July 28, 2017, https://blog.hubspot.com/sales/gratitude-journal.

9. "The Power of a Focused Life," Focus Course, https://thefocuscourse.com/course.

The 3rd Habit:
Preparation and Planning

1. Steven Pressfield, *The War of Art: Break Through the Blocks & Win Your Inner Creative Battles* (New York: Warner Books, 2003), 108.

2. Seth Godin, *Linchpin: Are You Indispensable?* (New York: Portfolio, 2011), 107.

3. Benedict XVI, "Address of His Holiness Benedict XVI to the Participants in a Course on the Internal Forum Organized by the Tribunal of the Apostolic Penitentiary," Libreria Editrice Vaticana, March 7, 2008, https://w2.vatican.va/content/benedictxvi/en/speeches/2008/march/documents/hf_ben-xvi_spe_20080307_penitenzieria-apostolica.html.

4. G. K. Chesterton, *The Ball and the Cross* (New York: John Lane, 1909), 227.

5. John Paul II, https://w2.vatican.va/content/john-paul-ii/en/speeches/1997/september/documents/hf_jp-ii_spe_19970927_youth-bologna.html.

6. David Allen, *Getting Things Done: The Art of Stress-Free Productivity* (New York: Penguin Books, 2015), 59.

The 4th Habit:
Persistence and Perseverance

1. Carol Dweck, *Mindset: The New Psychology of Success* (New York: Ballantine Books, 2007), 15.

2. Angela Duckworth et al., "Grit: Perseverance and Passion for Long-Term Goals," *Journal of Personality and Social Psychology* 92, no. 6 (July 2007): 1087–1101.

3. Angela Duckworth, *Grit: The Power of Passion and Perserver-ance* (New York: Scribner, 2016).

4. Amanda Ripley, *The Smartest Kids in the World: And How They Got That Way* (New York: Simon and Schuster, 2014), 154.

5. Benedict XVI, "General Audience," Libreria Editrice Vaticana, January 31, 2007, http://w2.vatican.va/content/benedict-xvi/en/audiences/2007/documents/hf_ben-xvi_aud_20070131.html.

6. Chris Lowney, *Everyone Leads: How to Revitalize the Catholic Church* (Lanham, MD: Rowman and Littlefield, 2017), 1.

The 5th Habit: Pondering

1. Courtney Seiter, "Inside the Buffer Retreat: How and Why We Spent $111,874 Meeting Face to Face," *Buffer* (blog), last modified August 5, 2015, https://open.buffer.com/inside-buffer-retreat.

2. Bob Frisch and Logan Chandler, "Off-Sites That Work," *Harvard Business Review* (June 2006), https://hbr.org/2006/06/off-sites-that-work.

3. *A Civil Action*, directed by Steven Zaillian (Burbank, CA: Touchstone Pictures, 1998).

4. Thomas Merton, *The Seven Storey Mountain* (New York: Mariner Books, 1999), 148.

5. "The Carmelite Spirituality of John Paul II," Order of Carmelites, http://ocarm.org/en/content/ocarm/carmelite-spirituality-john-paul-ii.

6. Dorothy Day, *The Duty of Delight: The Diaries of Dorothy Day*, ed. Robert Ellsberg (Milwaukee, WI: Marquette University Press, 2008), 15.

Conclusion:
Progress over Perfection

1. Terry Hershey, *The Power of Pause: Becoming More by Doing Less* (Chicago: Loyola Press, 2009),12.

RECOMMENDED RESOURCES

FOR BEGINNERS

Calvillo, David N. *Real Men Pray the Rosary: A Practical Guide to a Powerful Prayer*. Notre Dame, IN: Ave Maria Press, 2013.

Chole, Alicia Britt. *The Sacred Slow: A Holy Departure from Fast Faith*. Nashville: Thomas Nelson, 2017.

Eldredge, Becky. *Busy Lives and Restless Souls: How Prayer Can Help You Find the Missing Peace in Your Life*. Chicago: Loyola Press, 2017.

Foss, Elizabeth. *Ponder*. Charleston, SC: CreateSpace, 2018.

Hendey, Lisa M., and Sarah A. Reinhard. *The Catholic Mom's Prayer Companion: A Book of Daily Reflections*. Notre Dame, IN: Ave Maria Press, 2016.

Irish Jesuits. *Sacred Space: The Prayer Book 2019*. Chicago: Loyola Press, 2018.

Kelley, Matthew. *Rediscover the Rosary: The Modern Power of an Ancient Prayer*. New York: Beacon Publishing, 2017.

King, Heather. *Holy Desperation: Praying as If Your Life Depends on It*. Chicago: Loyola Press, 2017.

Libresco, Leah. *Arriving at Amen: Seven Catholic Prayers That Even I Can Offer*. Notre Dame, IN: Ave Maria Press, 2015.

Sri, Edward. *Praying the Rosary Like Never Before: Encounter the Wonder of Heaven and Earth.* Cincinnati, OH: Servant, 2017.

Wicks, Robert J. *Prayer in the Catholic Tradition: A Handbook of Practical Approaches.* Cincinnati, OH: Franciscan Media, 2016.

Williams, Mary. *The Examen Journal: Finding God Everyday.* Self-published, 2017.

FOR THOSE WITH SOME PRAYER EXPERIENCE

Bosio, John. *Joined by Grace: A Catholic Prayer Book for Married Couples.* Notre Dame, IN: Ave Maria Press, 2017.

Burke, Dan. *Into the Deep: Finding Peace through Prayer.* New York: Beacon Publishing, 2017.

Dees, Jared. *Praying the Angelus: Find Joy, Peace and Purpose in Everyday Life.* Notre Dame, IN: Ave Maria Press, 2017.

Glen, Genevieve. *Sauntering through Scripture: A Book of Reflections.* Collegeville, MN: Give Us This Day, 2018.

Huston, Paula. *By Way of Grace: Moving from Faithfulness to Holiness.* Chicago: Loyola Press, 2007.

Murphy, Charles M. *Eucharistic Adoration: Holy Hour Meditations on the Seven Last Words of Christ.* Notre Dame, IN: Ave Maria Press, 2012.

Muto, Susan. *Gratefulness: The Habit of a Grace-Filled Life.* Notre Dame, IN: Ave Maria Press, 2018.

O'Boyle, Donna Marie Cooper. *Catholic Saints Prayer Book: Moments of Inspiration from Your Favorite Saints.* Huntington, IN: Our Sunday Visitor, 2013.

Paintner, Christine Valters. *Lectio Divina—The Sacred Art: Transforming Words and Images into Heart-Centered Prayer.* Woodstock, VT: SkyLight Paths, 2011.

Thibodeaux, Mark E. *Reimagining the Ignatian Examen: Fresh Ways to Pray from Your Day.* Chicago: Loyola Press, 2015.

Tighe, Tommy. *The Catholic Hipster Handbook: Rediscovering Cool Saints, Forgotten Prayers, and Other Weird but Sacred Stuff.* Notre Dame, IN: Ave Maria Press, 2017.
Wicks, Robert J. *Prayerfulness: Awakening to the Fullness of Life.* Notre Dame, IN: Sorin Books, 2011.

FOR SEASONED PRAYER WARRIORS

Brother Lawrence. *The Practice of the Presence of God.* New Kensington, PA: Whitaker House, 1982.
Burns, John. *Lift Up Your Heart: A 10-Day Personal Retreat with St. Francis de Sales.* Notre Dame, IN: Ave Maria Press, 2017.
Day, Dorothy. *The Duty of Delight: The Diaries of Dorothy Day.* Edited by Robert Ellsberg. New York: Image, 2011.
Finley, James. *The Contemplative Heart.* Notre Dame, IN: Sorin Books, 1999.
Francis de Sales. *An Introduction to the Devout Life.* Charlotte, NC: TAN Books, 1994.
Malham, Joseph. *Drawing Closer to Christ: A Self-Guided Icon Retreat.* Notre Dame, IN: Ave Maria Press, 2017.
McColman, Carl. *Befriending Silence: Discovering the Gifts of Cistercian Spirituality.* Notre Dame, IN: Ave Maria Press, 2015.
Merton, Thomas. *New Seeds of Contemplation.* Cambridge, MA: New Direction Publishing, 2007.
Mother Teresa. *Come Be My Light: The Private Writings of the Saint of Calcutta.* Edited by Brian Kolodiejchuk. New York: Image, 2009.
Nouwen, Henri J. M. *With Open Hands.* Notre Dame, IN: Ave Maria Press, 2006.
Rolheiser, Ronald. *Prayer: Our Deepest Longing.* Cincinnati, OH: Franciscan Media, 2013.
Sarah, Robert. *The Power of Silence: Against the Dictatorship of Noise.* San Francisco: Ignatius Press, 2017.

Thérèse of Lisieux. *The Story of a Soul: The Autobiography of the Little Flower*. Charlotte, NC: TAN Books, 2010.

Urs von Balthasar, Hans. *Prayer*. San Francisco: Ignatius Press, 1986.

Michael St. Pierre is executive director of the Catholic Campus Ministry Association. He has more than twenty years of experience in parishes and schools and with nonprofit organizations as a teacher, campus minister, department chairman, youth minister, dean of students, and president.

His work has been featured on numerous podcasts, in various publications, and on radio, including *Catechist*, *Productive Magazine*, *America*, Relevant Radio, *Catholic School Matters*, *Today's Parish Minister*, *Give Us This Day*, *Momentum*, and *Catholic Exchange*.

St. Pierre and his wife, Cary, live with their children in New Jersey.

Facebook: mikekstpierre
Instagram: @mikekstpierre
Twitter: @mikekstpierre
www.mikestpierre.com

Chris Lowney is an author, speaker, leadership consultant, and chairman of the board of Catholic Health Initiatives.

AVE

Ave Maria Press

Founded in 1865, Ave Maria Press,
a ministry of the Congregation of
Holy Cross, is a Catholic publishing
company that serves the spiritual and
formative needs of the Church and its
schools, institutions, and ministers;
Christian individuals and families; and
others seeking spiritual nourishment.

For a complete listing of titles from

Ave Maria Press

Sorin Books

Forest of Peace

Christian Classics

visit avemariapress.com